Research Guide
to Religious Studies

Research Guide to Religious Studies

John F. Wilson and Thomas P. Slavens

SOURCES OF INFORMATION
IN THE HUMANITIES
NO. 1

American Library Association

1982

Sources of Information in the Humanities
Thomas P. Slavens, series editor

Designed by Harvey Retzloff

Composed by Automated Office Systems Inc.
in Sabon on a Text Ed/VIP
phototypesetting system

Printed on 50-pound Warren's 66, a pH-
neutral stock, and bound in
C-grade Holliston Roxite cloth
by Braun-Brumfield, Inc.

Library of Congress Cataloging in Publication Data

Wilson, John Frederick.
  Research guide to religious studies.

  (Sources of information in the humanities   ;   no. 1)
  Includes bibliographies and index.
  1. Religion—Methodology. 2. Religion—Bibliography.
I. Slavens, Thomas P., 1928– . II. Title.
III. Series.
BL41.W5   291'.072   81-22862
ISBN 0-8389-0330-4   AACR2

CONTENTS

PREFACE TO THE SERIES

The purpose of this series is to help librarians, students of library science, and other interested persons in the use of resources in the humanities. The series encompasses art, linguistics, literature, music, philosophy, and religion. These fields share an interest in the creative, aesthetic, and imaginative impulses of human beings and the cultures in which they live. Individuals find joy in music, art, and literature; others thoroughly enjoy discussing linguistics and philosophy; and a basic religious impulse has prompted the quest for emotional and intellectual fulfullment. Scholarship in the humanities has been produced with the goal of enhancing the quality of human life while seeking to understand it more adequately, and those who seek information about the humanities make use of libraries; often, however, they become confused by the large quantities of available materials.

This series, then, is intended as a guide in the search for information in the humanities. The series, as previously noted, consists of six titles covering art, linguistics, literature, music, philosophy, and religion. Each volume is divided into two parts. The first features a survey of the field by a specialist, and the second is an annotated list of major reference works. The survey includes a history of the field, a description of methodology, and current issues and research. The descriptions of issues and research summarize critical assessments of significant monographs, with an emphasis on modern scholarship. They do not cite primary sources, such as the Bible, Shakespeare's plays, music, or art. Rather, the essays focus on the concepts presented in key secondary works. They stress Western subjects and titles; in the case of literature, because of the mass of material available, the essays emphasize English literature. Citations are given in full following each section.

The second part of each volume lists and annotates major reference works. The list relates subject scholarship to bibliography, thus expediting information retrieval.

Many people have assisted in the preparation of this series. They include the Publishing Services staff of the American Library Association, without whose encouragement the series would not have been produced. The collaborators are also grateful for financial assistance from the University of Michigan which granted us the first Warner G. Rice Faculty Award in the Humanities for the purpose of assisting in the preparation of this book. These funds were used to employ Marjorie Corey, Anne Deason, Richard Heritage, Margaret Hillmer, Patricia Kirschner, Karen O'Donnell, and Robert Krupp as research assistants in this project; their endeavors are very much appreciated. We also take pleasure in thanking the professors who wrote the essays. They represent the best of humanistic scholarship in the United States and have made a major contribution to the organization of information in their disciplines.

THOMAS P. SLAVENS

PART I

INTRODUCTION
TO
RELIGIOUS
SCHOLARSHIP

1

The Study of Religion

The study of religion, also referred to as religious studies, is a scholarly inquiry into the religious aspects of human societies and the cultures associated with them. Accordingly it features systematic attention to a wide range of material. Such diverse topics as the following are included within its scope: cultic institutions dedicated to religious ends; patterns of religious authority and behavior that diverge markedly; conceptualizations of religious beliefs that vary widely; collections of religious meaning in relationship to given cultures; charismatic figures; and innovative movements with differing significance to larger societies.

Since religion as a particular subject is studied in its relationship to specific social and cultural contexts, several appropriate methods or approaches are useful. In general, however, historical, literary, and philosophical techniques or modes of inquiry predominate. Furthermore, by reason of its location in contemporary society, certain subject matters and the disciplines appropriate to their study have become especially central to the study of religion. Introductory sections of this essay comment on the emergence and development of interest in religion as a scholarly subject, and suggest the scope of the discussion that has evolved concerning its definition. Subsequent sections indicate historic focal points of work and areas of current emphasis in religion as a scholarly discipline. The major sections of the essay then review the chief fields of scholarship in religion, calling attention to subdivisions and current directions within each.

RELIGION AS A CONCEPT

The term *religion* probably derives from the Latin root *religare,*

3

"to bind." It was used sparingly in antiquity in several forms but its meaning in contemporary critical usage derives from the Enlightenment. Frank E. Manuel and Ernst Cassirer have identified this cultural shift and its implications for conceptualizing religion. In modern usage, the term identifies an interconnected set of beliefs and patterns of behavior (or rituals) that apparently express as a system the basic shape or texture of the culture or subculture under observation. Therefore in its contemporary usage religion has come to signify an abstraction from what is, in the first instance, a lived and comprehensive reality.

In this framework, religious materials are identified as particular activities within, or aspects of, culture distinguishable from others recognized as art, politics, science, or the like. Of course, each of these activities has become institutionalized and hence has a social base. Therefore religion is an intellectual construct corresponding to a particular set of social and cultural activities arrived at for purposes of critical analysis. While the resources of modern scholarship have been adapted to the study of this subject matter, it is necessary to emphasize that the modern concept of religion is itself the product of intellectual reflection upon cultural activities. Thus the modern conventional self-referential use of the term depends upon this analytical framework, derived from the Enlightenment.

One consequence of this fact is that religion, like other aspects of culture, is thought to be general or universal, so that comparison between cultures is broadly possible while, based on the skeptical conclusions reached by David Hume, it is also generally thought that the discovery of an "essence" of religion is impossible. Of course, such issues as the adequacy of particular conceptualizations of religion (a topic referred to later in this chapter) continue to hold interest. Once the understanding of religion as it was associated with the Enlightenment became common, however, religious study has been primarily cast in terms of historical data or empirical phenomena, rather than abstract philosophical claims or truth assertions. From such a perspective the historical development of particular religions has naturally received extensive attention as a function of cultural studies. Students of religion immediately learn, however, that even highly differentiated religious traditions may not be strictly comparable. For example, theological reflection has been thorough and systematic in Western Christianity, while it is difficult to identify a strictly equivalent activity as a pronounced aspect of the Islamic tradition. And Buddhist philosophical reflection is fundamentally nontheistic, in decided divergence from both the premises and the conclusions laboriously reached by classical Christian philosophers.

Because it is implicitly an intellectual counter, a second consequence to the use of religion as a concept is the argument that it is simply a reification, that substantiality is wrongly attributed to it as an intellectual category. In the conventional figure, religion is in the eye of the beholder only. Undoubtedly an important insight stands behind this argument, focusing on the active role of the mind in reducing all data to intelligibility; in such activity the possibilities for fundamental misinterpretation and overinterpretation are clear. But the skeptical insistence that this concept is a reification seems no more—or less—relevant to the study of religion than to the study of other differentiated aspects of cultures. In formal terms, the study of art, music, literature, and politics (to suggest only a few categories of cultural analysis rooted in the same Enlightenment soil as religion) are also subject to this criticism. The difference, of course, lies in questions of substance. Nonverifiable claims are made in particular religious traditions that have to do both with particular realities (e.g., the existence of God) and the general conditions of human life (e.g., universal depravity). From the point of view of religious study, the fact that these claims are made, and the particular forms given to them, constitutes the proper subject for analysis. In short, for the purposes of scholarship religious doctrines are comparable to a work of art; religious institutions are comparable to those found in the political arena.

Wilfred Cantwell Smith, in a sustained discussion, strongly asserts a different position on these questions. He explores the emergence of the modern use of the term "religion" in the seventeenth and eighteenth centuries, using his discoveries to vigorously argue the case that the term is inadequate as a generic concept. In his judgment it cannot intellectually embrace, and thus effectively comprehend, the diverse pieties and beliefs characteristic of different human cultures. He further argues in his study that, as a reified term, religion entails a theoretical framework that finally obscures more than it discloses about the data it is intended to illuminate. As a consequence, Smith proposes that the concept religion be dropped altogether. Positively he prefers to use the self-referential terms "believers" and "behavers" for those, in diverse cultures, who adhere to and practice various traditions in faith.

This position is useful because it explicitly locates the importance of the Enlightenment for the study of religion in particular—and cultural studies in general. The premise of Smith's position, however, is that the motivation for the study of religion ought to be an advancement in dialogue or understanding between those in different traditions. The study of religion may, indeed, be instrumental to such an outcome, and enhanced understanding between traditions may provide a sense of purpose for scholars of religion. It does not, however, represent the justification for religious study. Nor does such an approach to the study of religion take into account the impulse to analyze cultures under a variety of formalities (in addition to religion), either by means of direct comparison or through broadly analytical frameworks. This latter program, in concert with parallel scholarly undertakings in other humanities and social sciences disciplines, is the explicit purpose of studying religion.

In this sense, the study of religion derives from the same intellectual sources that have been developed by modern scholars to understand other aspects of the world. This comprehensive scholarly enterprise proceeds through the formalities of academic disciplines as reflected in the faculties of universities and the internal divisions of college curriculums. Accordingly it is imperative to recognize that while scholars of religion have wide-ranging interests in diverse cultures, and although their energies are directed to a variety of historical epochs, the objectives they seek (the analysis of religious materials) and the procedures they utilize (the various appropriate disciplines) are thoroughly "modern." Therefore it is a fundamental error to construe the study of religion or religious studies as the attempt to simply preserve, continue, or perfect ancient traditions or modern patterns of faith and practice in their own terms. Scholarly study of religion is rooted in modern culture and determined by its premises in exactly the same way that critical studies of economics, politics, history, literature, art, music, and comparable subject matters have developed in the last several centuries. For this reason alone, the problem of the definition of religion must receive attention at an early stage of this essay.

At the same time, however, the study of religion is not entirely parallel to the critical studies of other aspects of a culture. What does set scholarly studies of religion apart from other comparable activities is the antiquity and vigor of the prior traditions of learning that were closely linked to dominant Western religious communities. In the West, at least since classical antiquity, scholarly reflection was appropriated to the purposes of Jewish and Christian religious communities—indeed, actively carried on within them. Therefore the modern interest in the study of religion, which had its decisive origin in the Enlightenment, has had to relate to already existing, indeed distinguished, scholarly traditions sustained within particular communities. Of course this necessity is not altogether unique to religious study; for example, systematic reflection on political philosophy, often in conjunction with interest in political regimes as well as religious traditions, also began in ancient times, and modern critical scholarship directed to such aspects of culture also has had to incorporate traditions of learning that antedate the Enlightenment. But in the case of no other discipline are these traditions of learning so vigorous, or so directly linked to institutional structures of authority (such as ecclesiastical bodies) within the general society. Of course, strong and vital churchly traditions of scholarship often remain active in the contemporary world.

Therefore the study of religion at the present time embodies two strands: (1) a strand of scholarship that has continued antecedent traditions of learning, especially involving Judaism and Christianity—themselves also vitally affected by the second strand, (2) a more generic scholarly interest in religion. One purpose of this essay is to trace, through contemporary scholarship, at least some of the numerous patterns established by these strands, singly and in combination. To unravel them is neither altogether possible nor necessarily desirable. This consideration of the unique pattern of religious scholarship indicates a powerful reason for turning attention to the basic question of the definition of religion.

DEFINING RELIGION

Modern definitions of religion are so numerous and varied that this situation in itself has led to questions about the validity of the concept. Several comments are in order. First, agreement upon precise definitions of other cultural subjects, such as politics or literature, is probably as difficult theoretically, if not so apparent practically. Second, in a field that appears to utilize an agreed-upon working definition, such as art or music, that same apparent consensus often depends upon acceptance of high cultural materials as controlling factors in the determination of the definition. In such cases, the fact that popular cultural materials may also require serious analytical study under the same rubric is an issue often evaded. Further, when determined by the standards of high culture, a given definition may work less well for the study of essentially mixed data. On these grounds, therefore, the concept religion is formally parallel to other concepts.

Some definitions of religion are attempts to suggest the intensity and uniqueness of reflection upon life within a culture from the participant's point of view. An example would be Alfred North Whitehead's classic dictum, "religion is what an individual does with his solitariness." Such a position is thoroughly consistent with W. C. Smith's argument, previously suggested, that religion is reified when interpreted as if it identified a given objective reality. From this point of view religion only exists, so to speak, through the faith of those who act on its basis. At another extreme is the type of interpretation given to religion by the influential French sociologist, Emile Durkheim. In his perspective, religion has to do most basically with human collectivities. More precisely, it is the means through which a society presents itself—that is to say, orders life so as to overcome the potential chaos that is an ever-present threat.

In terms of the study of religion this latter perspective, which emphasizes the collective aspects of religion, is much more significant than those perspectives that give primary attention to individual or personal experience as the starting point for analysis. It should be clear, of course, that even such seemingly opposed definitions are linked together through recognition that there is a basic human impulse to give order to the world. This is necessary so that culture is protected against chaos, life routinized at its center as well as secured at its outer reaches, and the ever-present uncertainties of experience rendered tolerable, if not explained in a cosmic framework. In this deep sense, all serious attempts at a definition of religion understand that it exercises on behalf of its adherents a kind of power that is ultimate or cosmic in human terms, because it is power with respect to the framework of human behavior and belief. This does not mean religions are primarily concerned with ultimate powers while other cultural activities concern mundane powers only. Rather, the primary religious issue is the basic ordering of experience, especially collective experience, often in terms of reference points behind or beyond it; naturally the symbols under which that is done and the ceremonies through which it is achieved vary widely. Perspectives on religion that start from "inside" the experience, as well as those that derive from "outside" observations (interpreting religion in social as well as individual terms) certainly share this understanding of why particular cultural activities are usefully considered as religious. In general, the latter (or observer's) framework has more direct bearing on scholarship in the field because the interpretation of religious materials in cultural settings marks out the special subfields and the formal disciplines reflected in the literature here under review. But definitions of religion that emphasize experience, collective as well as personal, do lead back to the same point by the means suggested above.

In the development of religious scholarship in the nineteenth century, the issue of definition was linked to the emergence of the numerous "schools" that rested upon competing theories of religion. For example, Max Müller stands as founder of the philosophical and comparative mythological school in the history of religions. Subsequently, ethnological interests, followed by sociological and psychological interpretations, prevailed. In some ways the most useful means of contemporary access to this rich discussion is provided in a reader compiled by William Lessa and Evon Z. Vogt.

Against this background, recent symbolic anthropology has rendered extremely useful service to the study of religion as a result of the attention that has been given to the understanding of contemporary cultures as wholes, with religion a recognizable aspect of them. This approach has had the advantage of highlighting the interdependence of theory and data, or interpretation and evidence. Because anthropologists have insisted that culture be studied in its entirety, the recognition given to the place of religion within culture has been extremely useful as a theoretical contribution to religious studies. Of course anthropologists vary widely among themselves in terms of the particular premises and formulations they use, but the breadth and intensity of interest in religion, or some aspects of it, on the part of contemporary cultural anthropologists is not in doubt.

Possibly the formulation most widely appropriated by religion scholars is that developed by Clifford Geertz. Offering theoretical statements of great power and demonstrating the utility of his approach through studies of specific cultural materials, he has played an enormously influential role in current discussions about religion. Mary Douglas has also stimulated a great deal of interest on the basis of her proposals about the relationship between cosmologies and social structures, giving ample attention to religious beliefs and actions. A somewhat different approach has been offered by Anthony F. C. Wallace, who has insisted upon the internal complexity of religious systems as a fundamental characteristic. These contributions by cultural anthropologists to discussions of religion are interesting examples of cross-fertilization between cognate fields—such as occurs more frequently in the natural sciences, possibly, than in the humanities and social sciences.

In varying combinations, the foregoing authors interpret religion within frames of reference or frameworks of inquiry first developed by Emile Durkheim and Max Weber, whose legacies to modern social science are widely recognized. Emile Durkheim's influence stems especially from a major monograph on *The Elementary Forms of the Religious Life*. Although Durkheim noted periods of social effervescence, and the special role of religion in them, he held a particularly strong interest in the contribution religion makes to stable social orders. By contrast, Max Weber was especially intrigued with the genesis of the modern world. He thus took the question of social change—that is, how modern society came into being—as basic, and he developed a specialized interest in the roles religion might have played in such changes. This problematic supported his important study *The Protestant Ethic and the Spirit of Capitalism* and also may be detected in the materials brought together in his *Sociology of Religion*. Additional comments on related issues will be found below under the heading "The Scientific Study of Religion," and specific discussion of the literature is given in appropriate sections of the companion volume, *Sources of Information in the Social Sciences*, edited by Carl M. White.

DEVELOPMENT OF THE FIELD OF RELIGIOUS SCHOLARSHIP

Religion or religious studies has developed self-conscious direction as a field of scholarship in American institutions of higher education, especially over the last thirty years (broadly since World War II). This self-consciousness is in part a result of its recency, but it primarily stems from the fact that the study of religion has also comprehended, along with the post-Enlightenment interest in religion, sensitivity to the scholarly traditions of antiquity and distinction. Prominent among these traditions have been more strictly theological scholarship in the various Roman Catholic and Protestant versions of Christianity, as well as the traditions of learning within other communities of faith, in particular Judaism, Hinduism, and Buddhism. The ways in which the older traditions of scholarship have been appropriated into the study of religion vary, as well as the degrees of their transformation on the one hand, and their continuation as independent schools of scholarship on the other. Relevant sections in the subsequent discussion of particular subfields will include comments about older patterns of scholarship and their relationships to contemporary religious studies.

At this point, it is important to establish the more general observation by calling attention to the fundamental institutional location in which the study of religion is systematically pursued at the present time. Within the last three decades, scholarship in religion has become increasingly associated with the arts and science faculties of universities and with liberal arts colleges. A volume edited by Paul Ramsey and John F. Wilson at the end of the 1960s provides an overview of this issue and suggests the range of scholarship associated with religion in arts and science locations. Particular essays summarize the status of subfields and also serve to delineate the inclusive range of religious studies. (An earlier study of scholarship in religion edited by Ramsey is also relevant.) A slight volume by Ninian Smart, who pioneered the development of religious studies in the United Kingdom, represents a very useful discussion of the scholarly study of religion as a polymethodic science analyzing cultural materials in the setting of contemporary society. It may be interesting to note, however, that the formal case for study of religion within American universities was fully developed as early as the beginning of this century when the modern differentiation of academic disciplines was taking place. While the case then made by Morris Jastrow now seems self-evident, actual development of the field was slow.

In many respects, the best available indexes of the vitality of a scholarly field are in the activity of professional societies and the quality of journals. In the case of religion, distinctions must be drawn between the overall field and the various subfields. In appropriate sections of this essay attention will be given to relevant specialized professional societies and journals that represent ongoing scholarly activity with respect to religion. As far as the overall field goes, the post-World War II period is notable. First, with respect to professional societies, an older and relatively limited organization was revitalized as the American Academy of Religion—broadly comparable to field-embracing professional societies such as the Modern Language Association, the American Historical Association, or the American Political Science Association. Its annual meeting draws participants from throughout North America. In structure, the programs are divided along the general lines of the subfields discussed later in this essay. In addition, regional bodies of the academy sponsor annual meetings. A second field-encompassing professional development is represented by the founding of an umbrella organization to facilitate activities within and between the numerous specialized professional organizations: the Council on the Study of Religion. Encouraged by the American Council of Learned Societies and other well-established groups, the council has served an important function simply through symbolizing that there is a common field of interest in the scholarly study of religion. Numerous additional specialized societies will be discussed at appropriate points in this essay.

A second index exists in the publications that represent routine means of communication within scholarly fields. As in the case of professional societies, attention will be given at appropriate points in the following sections to journals that serve particular subfields. But several publications are sufficiently field-encompassing to receive notice here. The American Academy of Religion sponsors a quarterly *Journal* that presents both important general essays and field-specific pieces of interest to members throughout the overall organization. The *Journal* recently experimented with a publishing format comparable to that of some science fields. Most of the articles were published as abstracts only, full separates being available on demand or by standing order. Inadequate reponse has led to a return to the more conventional publishing program. The Council on the Study of Religion also sponsors a comprehensive reviewing organ for the field as a whole, *Religious Studies Review*. An independent development has been the emergence of Scholars Press as an ambitious vehicle to facilitate scholarly publication of journals and monographs, as well as circulation of existing material. Scholars Press has cooperated with several professional societies in addition to the ones strictly concerned with the study of religion or some subfield of it—such as the American Philological Association.

THE SHAPE OF THE SCHOLARLY STUDY OF RELIGION

The extreme positions in the definition of religion have been previously noted, from Whitehead's religion as what an individual does with his solitariness to Durkheim's religion as symbolization of the collectivity as reality. This polarity suggests a formulation that may help in achieving a basic understanding of the state of current scholarship in religion. The scholarly study of religion might be portrayed as a spectrum between two end points, or likened to an elongated elipse with the separate foci near or at extreme limits. One pole represents interest in the materials of religion as given in cultural settings: particular, unique, requiring critical study in the appropriate context. The other pole represents concern for religion in the intellectual and emotional experience(s) of humans as individuals and in groups, that is to say, how it organizes life as a fundamental means of self-understanding. Alternatively poles might also be thought of as an objective, critical or outside view of religion and a subjective, empathetic or inside perspective. In some sense, current study of religion exists in relationship to both of these poles. In yet another image, the scholarly study of religion moves within the two dimensions associated with these interests, and particular scholarship is located in various positions between them. Some kinds of studies are very closely controlled by the objective or critical pole; others are almost exclusively oriented to the subjective. Virtually all scholarship in religion, however, takes account of both dimensions although in significantly different proportions.

This bipolarity or two dimensionality is basic to religious studies as a field of scholarship. In the absence of appreciation for such nuances, especially when there is vigorous assertion that one pole is primary, scholarship related to the other dimension or pole appears as a diversion from appropriate pursuits. This distortion can occur with respect to either one of these dimensions. When the subjective or inside perspective dominates, as may easily occur in the setting of a particular tradition, religious study tends to emphasize interests derived from a particular theological subject, or the self-understanding of a given religious community, or the intensity or idiosyncrasy of personal experience. Under these circumstances, critical, historical, philosophical criteria (that is to say, scholarly scientific concerns generally) can recede very much into the background. By contrast, when the objective pole is stressed, as usually occurs in university contexts, scholarly study moves toward other arts and science disciplines, including especially historical, literary, philosophical, and sociological studies. Under these conditions, the interior or subjective and more explicitly religious interests may cease to be sharply focused and in the extreme case disappear from the field of inquiry.

Because the field of religious study displays these bifold characteristics, it is more readily possible to delineate the subfields of religious study than necessarily to identify their interrelationships. By deliberate design this essay will be organized so that discussion will move from giving attention to subfields in which greater emphasis falls on religious scholarship under the strong influence of the objective pole, or critical accounts of religion, to those in which more emphasis is given to the subjective pole, or inquiry is controlled in decisive ways by commitment to a religion or emphasis upon the experience of it. Thus, the discussion begins with a review of those aspects of the field that explicitly aim to achieve a comprehensive study of religion as a part of human social orders and moves toward, albeit not in linear fashion, concluding sections on those subfields that emphasize more tradition-directed scholarly concerns in the West.

In general, the subfields controlled by the objective pole derive from the Enlightenment interest in religion as a cultural phenomenon, that is to say, as phenomena in other cultures, while the subfields at the other end of the spectrum depart from that commitment to learning which is internal to a specific religious tradition. But this is not a rigorous distinction. Critical modes of scholarship have been appropriated by at least some of the positive traditions and are directed consistently at the materials of given traditions. On the other side, philosophical clarification of the problematic represented by religion has introduced the issue of subjectivity at the center of critical analysis of religion. Thus movement along this spectrum, or between these poles, will be notably crablike. The essay will also call attention to numerous subfields and specific points of interest where adjacencies to scholarly inquiries strictly outside the formal study of religion consistently impinge directly upon religion scholarship per se.

Alston, William P. "Religion." In *The Encyclopedia of Philosophy*, ed. by Paul Edwards. Vol. 7. New York: Macmillan, 1967.

Cassirer, Ernst. *The Philosophy of the Enlightenment*. Princeton, N.J.: Princeton Univ. Pr., 1951.

Douglas, Mary. *Cultural Bias*. London: Royal Anthropological Institute, 1978 (Occasional Paper no. 34).

———. *Natural Symbols: Explorations in Cosmology*. New York: Vintage, 1973.

Durkheim, Emile. *The Elementary Forms of the Religious Life*. Tr. by J. W. Swaim. New York: Macmillan, 1915.

Geertz, Clifford. "Religion as a Cultural System." In *The Interpretation of Cultures*. New York: Basic Books, 1973.

Jastrow, Morris. *The Study of Religion*. New York: Scribner's, 1908. Repr.: Chico, Calif.: American Academy of Religion, 1981.

Lessa, William, and Evon Z. Vogt, eds. *Reader in Comparative Religion: An Anthropological Approach*. 3d ed. New York: Harper & Row, 1972.

Manuel, Frank E. *The Eighteenth Century Confronts the Gods*. Cambridge, Mass.: Harvard Univ. Pr., 1959.

Ramsey, Paul, ed. *Religion*. Englewood Cliffs, N.J.: Prentice-Hall, 1965.

——— and John F. Wilson, eds. *The Study of Religion in Colleges and Universities*. Princeton, N.J.: Princeton Univ. Pr., 1970.

Smart, Ninian. *The Science of Religion and the Sociology of Knowledge*. Princeton, N.J.: Princeton Univ. Pr., 1973.

Smith, Wilfred Cantwell. *The Meaning and End of Religion*. New York: Macmillan, 1963.

Wach, Joachim. *Types of Religious Experience*. Chicago, Univ. of Chicago Pr., 1951.

Wallace, Anthony F. C. *Religion: An Anthropological View*. New York: Random House, 1966.

Weber, Max. *The Protestant Ethic and the Spirit of Capitalism*. Tr. by Talcott Parsons. London: Allen & Unwin, 1930.

Whitehead, Alfred North. *Religion in the Making*. Cambridge, Mass.: Harvard Univ. Pr., 1927.

2

History
of Religions

Especially in Great Britain and the United States, the phrase "history of religions" has become the designation for what Europeans think of as the scientific study of religion; the term used by continental scholars is "Religionswissenschaft." As a general cultural science, the history of religions has been deeply influenced by a number of figures, most with roots in German academies. For example, the "father" of the discipline in England, Max Müller, taught at Oxford during the second half of the nineteenth century after migrating from Germany. His notable achievement was to develop a fifty-volume collection of sacred books of the East in translation and with introductions, making Eastern scriptures accessible to the Western world. More recently, Joachim Wach brought the fruits of continental scholarship to his American appointments—first at Brown University and, in the culmination of his career, at the University of Chicago. Mircea Eliade's long, full, and distinguished career represents in the same way the direct links between the history of religions in European and American scholarship.

This essay does not seek to review in detail the continental schools concerned with the general study of religion. Broadly independent traditions of scholarly inquiry are well established within each of the national communities, and not surprisingly national patterns of concentration upon selected cultural areas are pronounced. For instance, Dutch scholarship has placed special emphasis upon study of religion in classical antiquity; an international journal, *Numen*, is a central organ for this school. African cultures and those of the Indian subcontinent have held more interest for the British. French scholarship has traditionally directed attention to Southeast Asian and African societies. The special contribution of American history of religions in this respect may well be the consistent attention it has directed to religion in East Asian cultures, especially China and Japan. Thus, while the history of religions is self-consciously an international (albeit basically European and North American) community of scholarship, it nonetheless manifests a special emphasis in each nation.

In recent years in the United States and Canada, the history of religions has been increasingly influenced by a separate though cognate intellectual tradition, one developed as cultural or symbolic anthropology. The preceding section has already included references to the significant attention to the definition of religion found in anthropological literature, with important contributions by Mary Douglas, Clifford Geertz, and Anthony Wallace among the many who have offered significant formulations. Victor Turner is another anthropologist whose writings have been widely used by historians of religion; frequently his conceptualizations have been directly appropriated into current history of religions work. In addition, several other schools that have contributed to recent methodological reflection in this field should be identified. One is the intellectual concerns transferred from philosophical phenomenology, which has significantly developed the ideas of Edward Husserl, a continental philosophical phenomenologist. A second is the extremely influential structuralist program of Claude Lévi-Strauss. Historians of religion have not, of course, been the only specialists making use of these related academic traditions.

The history of religions does represent that concentration or field of religious study that is systematically directed to the study of religion as an identifiable dimension or aspect of human life. Under its formality, the human species is viewed as *homo religiosus*, that is to say, it is assumed that this dimension will appear under many permutations in various cultures. Thus one aspect or field of religious study is systematically oriented to the importance of both the nature of this dimension or side of human life and its characteristics. In the comprehensive studies of Joachim Wach, or in a widely used volume by Van der Leeuw originating in the Dutch tradition, it is possible to find this program worked out with vigor in detail. Mircea Eliade's many studies are no less informed by a comprehensive vision, although taken singly the early ones were less ambitious. In the quarterly journal *History of Religions*, these theoretical interests are under continuing discussion—albeit seldom reaching firm consensus. A comparable journal, *Religion*, has been published in Great Britain since 1970.

But the history of religions is not simply a theoretical science. It also identifies attempts to make use of the frameworks of interpretation derived from such theoretical considerations—in the extreme the postulate of *homo religiosus*—to study the religiously rich life of the human species. In this sense, the history of religions is frequently used as a less restricted designation. It serves as a general rubric under which numerous scholars have worked through a number of particular modalities to study a great variety of religious traditions ranging from the so-called primitive to such philosophically refined traditions as that found in Mahayana Buddhism. While not dichotomous, these two significations of history of religions as a rubric should be kept clearly in mind to avoid unnecessary confusion.

In the following sections, attention will be called to those literatures that have explored particular religions in various cultural settings. The major religious traditions of the globe, generally excluding Judaism and Christianity, are one set. Another long-standing component of the history of religions has been the attention directed at the religions of classical antiquity in the Mediterranean basin. A third is religions among pre-literate peoples or primitive religion. In addition, a striking innovation has been the concerted attempt within the last decade to use the history of religions approaches, initially developed and refined in application to alien cultures, to illuminate materials more strictly Western and contemporary. Each of these scholarly subjects will receive notice later in this essay.

But emphasis must now be given to another point: the history of religions may fail as a general science. While in one sense it represents a sustained attempt to achieve a generic science of religion, it has been previously noted that by the accident of its forms of development it has had especially strong ties to specific schools of philosophy and their programs. Further, it has been applied more consistently to certain traditions or ranges of religious belief and behavior than others, so that comparable attention has not been given to religion in various cultures. For example, the early emphasis upon sacred books, derived from Max Müller, committed the history of religions to studying literate societies and elite traditions. In this particular, the more recent use of folklorist studies, the incorporation of anthropological perspectives, and especially the influential work of Mircea Eliade, have significantly enriched the general history of religions program. But the point must be made that, in practice as well as theory, it has fallen short of representing that general science of religion that its partisans aspire for it to achieve and that its designation might suggest. This is one illustration of why the bifold character of religious scholarship has been stressed, as there is no firm consensus within religious scholarship at large about the theoretical position of history of religions as a general science.

De Vries, Jan. *The Study of Religion, a Historical Approach.* New York: Harcourt, Brace, 1967.
Eliade, Mircea. *The Myth of the Eternal Return.* New York: Pantheon Books, 1965.
————. *Patterns in Comparative Religion.* New York: World, 1972.
————. *The Sacred and the Profane: The Nature of Religion.* Tr. by Willard R. Trask. New York: Harcourt, Brace, 1959.
History of Religions. Chicago: University of Chicago, 1962– .
Kitagawa, Joseph M.; M. Eliade, and C. Long, eds. *The History of Religions: Essays on the Problem of Understanding.* Chicago: Univ. of Chicago Pr., 1967.
Otto, Rudolph. *The Idea of the Holy: An Inquiry into the Non-Rational Factor in the Idea of the Divine and Its Relation to the Rational.* 2d ed. Tr. by John Harvey. London: Oxford Univ. Pr., 1950.
Religion: A Journal of Religion and Religions. London: Kegan Paul, 1970– .
Turner, Victor. *The Forest of Symbols: Aspects of Ndembu Ritual.* Ithaca, N.Y.: Cornell Univ. Pr., 1967.
Van der Leeuw, G. *Religion in Essence and Manifestation.* London: Allen & Unwin, 1938.
Waardenburg, Jacques. *Classical Approaches to the Study of Religion.* The Hague, Paris: Mouton, 1973.
Wach, Joachim. *The Comparative Study of Religions.* New York: Columbia Univ. Pr., 1958.

RELIGION AMONG PRE-LITERATE PEOPLES

As noted in the preceding discussion, in many respects the development of the history of religions has been in terms of elaborating a theoretical construct of religion as a general aspect of culture. This objective has led to attempts to interpret the religious aspects of prehistoric societies, frequently on the basis of archeological data. The following studies, among many, in whole or part suggest the resources available: Joseph Campbell, *The Masks of God* (1959); E. O. James, *The Cult of the Mother-Goddess* (1959); Sibylle von Cles-Reden, *The Realm of the Great Goddess* (1962); and E. E. Jensen, *Myth and Cult among Primitive People* (1963).

Religion in pre-literate cultures has been a subject of continuing importance within cultural anthropology. For an elegant review of various proposals that have sought to explain its genesis and continued importance, see E. E. Evans-Pritchard, *Theories of Primitive Religion* (1965). Some older comprehensive discussions may be useful: Paul Radin, *Primitive Religion, Its Nature and Origin* (1937) and Wilson Dallam Wallis, *Religion in Primitive Society* (1939). The first emphasized the coinherence or interpenetration of religion with other aspects of such cultures, as well as the important role played by religious formulators or priest-thinkers. Wallis based his discussion on the dichotomous categories of the sacred and the profane as common to cultures, and the identification of supernatural forces as explanation for otherwise inexplicable phenomena. More recent general discussions are also available. Edward Norbeck, *Religion in Primitive Society* (1961) also utilizes the distinction between nature and supernature as his basic classification system. An explicitly functionalist or structural-functional approach may be reviewed in William J. Goode, *Religion among the Primitives* (1951).

African societies have presented an unusual opportunity for historians of religion. Religious aspects of the societies have been extensively discussed in recent literature. For overviews from somewhat different perspectives see E. Geoffrey Parrinder, *Religion in Africa* (1969) and Benjamin C. Ray, *African Religions: Symbol, Ritual and Community* (1976). T. O. Ranger and Isaria Kimambo edited an extensive series of essays that forms an important collection in their *The Historical Study of African Religion* (1972).

Historians of religion have been intensely concerned with ethnographic reports from pre-literate cultural areas, since they provide a relevant subject matter. Certain broad topics constitute focal points for ongoing scholarly discussion of religious questions. One focus has been an interest in mythic materials. Mircea Eliade has taken a broadly historical approach to the appreciation of myths. For his presentation of myths from separate cultures, see a large reader, *From Primitives to Zen* (1967). Of course, the work of Claude Lévi-Strauss has had enormous impact on these discussions through the development of structural linguistics; see his *Structural Anthropology* (1963). Specifically cosmic myths are discussed in Charles H. Long, *Alpha: The Myths of Creation* (1963).

A second focus of discussion has been the dominant religious figure. In this connection the shaman, one capable of ecstatic experience relevant to the collectivity, is extremely significant. See Mircea Eliade, *Shamanism: Archaic Technique of Ecstasy* (1964) as a basic study. Concern for health and the practice of healing is common to pre-literate cultures; see W. T. Corlett, *The Medicine-man of the American Indian and His Cultural Background* (1935); Sir Richard Winstedt, *The Malay Magician* (1951); and E. E. Evans-Pritchard, *Witchcraft, Oracles and Magic among the Azandi* (1937). As well, political leadership often is thought to embody divinity; for a representative discussion, see Olof Pettersson, *Chiefs and Gods: Religious and Social Elements in the South Eastern Bantu Kingship* (1953).

A third basic topic in scholarly discussions concerns cult institutions and ritual observances. Among general resources, see the following: John Middleton (editor), *Gods and Rituals: Readings in Religious Beliefs and Practices* (1967); Paul Radin, *The Road of Life and Death: A Ritual Drama of the American Indians* (1945); Victor W. Turner, *The Forest of Symbols* (1967); and Frank W. Young, *Initiation Ceremonies* (1965). The discussion of initiation rituals has now become a central concern in studying religion. The subject was first systematically considered by Arnold van Gennep in his *The Rites of Passage* (1960), originally published in 1908. In this connection, Victor W. Turner's work has been especially significant. See his *The Ritual Process: Structure and Anti-structure* (1969), and *Dramas, Fields, and Metaphors: Symbolic Action in Human Society* (1974). Readers may also wish to consult Eliade's *Birth and Rebirth* (1958).

These various kinds of studies in religious aspects of pre-literate cultures have made detailed use of ethnographic reports. In this sense they have derived from modern, critical scholarly approaches to these societies as self-contained systems. But there has been another level of interaction with pre-literate cultures too, that of responses on the part of those cultures to modernizing forces and their impact on the societies. In this connection, scholars have identified and studied the religious transformations (among others) of the pre-literate cultures. Generally the terms "millenarian movement" or "cargo cult" have been used to designate these cultural interactions with modernity.

The following studies are directed to one or more different cultural areas as indicated: Oceania, Kenelm Burridge, *New Heaven, New Earth* (1969); Melanesia, Peter Worsley, *The Trumpet Shall Sound: A Study of "Cargo" Cults of Melanesia* (1957); general, Vittorio Lanternari, *The Religions of the Oppressed* (1963); native American, Weston La Barre, *The Ghost Dance* (1970) and J. S. Slotkin, *The Peyote Religion* (1956); and comprehensive, Bryan R. Wilson, *Magic and the Millennium* (1973). I. C. Jarvie discusses the significance of this new topic in *The Revolution in Anthropology* (1967).

Burridge, Kenelm. *New Heaven, New Earth: A Study of Millenarian Activities*. New York: Schocken Books, 1969.
Campbell, Joseph. *The Masks of God*. New York: Viking, 1959.
Cles-Reden, Sibylle, von. *The Realm of the Great Goddess*. Englewood Cliffs, N.J.: Prentice-Hall, 1962.
Corlett, W. T. *The Medicine-man of the American Indian and His Cultural Background*. Springfield, Ill.: C. C. Thomas, 1935.
Eliade, Mircea. *Birth and Rebirth: The Religious Meanings of Initiation in Human Culture*. Tr. by W. R. Trask. New York: Harper & Row, 1958.
———. *From Primitives to Zen: A Thematic Sourcebook of the History of Religions*. New York: Harper & Row, 1967.
———. *Shamanism: Archaic Technique of Ecstasy*. Tr. by W. R. Trask. New York: Pantheon Books, 1964.
Evans-Pritchard, E. E. *Theories of Primitive Religion*. Oxford: Clarendon Pr., 1965.
———. *Witchcraft, Oracles and Magic among the Azandi*. Oxford: Clarendon Pr., 1937.
Goode, William J. *Religion among the Primitives*. Glencoe, Ill.: Free Pr., 1951.
James, E. O. *The Cult of the Mother-Goddess*. London: Thames & Hudson, 1959.
Jarvie, I. C. *The Revolution in Anthropology*. London: Routledge, 1967.
Jensen, E. E. *Myth and Cult among Primitive People*. Chicago: Univ. of Chicago Pr., 1963.
La Barre, Weston. *The Ghost Dance: Origins of Religion*. Garden City, N.Y.: Doubleday, 1970.
Lanternari, Vittorio. *The Religions of the Oppressed: A Study of Modern Messianic Cults*. Tr. by Lisa Sergio. New York: Knopf, 1963.
Lévi-Strauss, Claude. *Structural Anthropology*. Tr. by Claire Jacobson and Brooke Grundfest Schoepf. New York: Basic Books, 1963.
Long, Charles H. *Alpha: The Myths of Creation*. New York: Braziller, 1963.
Middleton, John, ed. *Gods and Rituals: Readings in Religious Beliefs and Practices*. New York: Natural History Pr., 1967.
Norbeck, Edward. *Religion in Primitive Society*. New York: Harper & Row, 1961.
Parrinder, E. Geoffrey. *Religion in Africa*. Harmondsworth, England: Penguin, 1969.
Pettersson, Olof. *Chiefs and Gods: Religious and Social Elements in the South Eastern Bantu Kingship*. Lund: Gleerup, 1953.
Radin, Paul. *Primitive Religion: Its Nature and Origin*. New York: Viking, 1937.
———. *The Road of Life and Death: A Ritual Drama of the American Indians*. New York: Pantheon, 1945.
Ranger, T. O., and Isaria Kimambo, eds. *The Historical Study of African Religion*. London: Heinemann, 1972.
Ray, Benjamin C. *African Religions: Symbol, Ritual and Community*. Englewood Cliffs, N.J.: Prentice-Hall, 1976.
Slotkin, J. S. *The Peyote Religion: A Study in Indian-White Relations*. Glencoe, Ill.: Free Pr., 1956.

Turner, Victor W. *Dramas, Fields, and Metaphors: Symbolic Action in Human Society*. Ithaca, N.Y.: Cornell Univ. Pr., 1974.

———. *The Forest of Symbols: Aspects of Ndembu Ritual*. Ithaca, N.Y.: Cornell Univ. Pr., 1967.

———. *The Ritual Process: Structure and Anti-structure*. Chicago: Aldine, 1969.

Van Gennep, Arnold. *The Rites of Passage.* (1908.) Tr. by Monika B. Vizdom and Gabrielle L. Caffee. Chicago: Univ. of Chicago Pr., 1960.

Wallis, Wilson Dallam. *Religion in Primitive Society*. New York: Crofts, 1939.

Wilson, Bryan R. *Magic and the Millennium: A Sociological Study of Religious Movements of Protest among Tribal and Third-World Peoples*. London: Heinemann, 1973.

Winstedt, Richard. *The Malay Magician: Being Shaman, Saira and Sufi*. London: Routledge & Paul, 1951.

Worsley, Peter. *The Trumpet Shall Sound: A Study of "Cargo" Cults in Melanesia*. London: Macgibbon & Kee, 1957.

Young, Frank W. *Initiation Ceremonies*. Indianapolis, Ind.: Bobbs-Merrill, 1965.

INDIAN RELIGIOUS TRADITIONS AND HINDUISM

Broad and inclusive patterns of myths and practices have been central to the cultural life of the Indian subcontinent for millennia. (On this point see W. Norman Brown's *Man in the Universe: Some Cultural Continuities in India* [1970].) It is unfortunate that the word "tradition" is unreflectively applied to these materials, since in the West this term connotes far more intellectual coherence and support from institutional authority than is applicable to the Indian situation. Furthermore, in historical terms these materials stand "behind" Buddhism, as its source; they were also certainly carried into Southeast Asia. They doubtless influenced in decisive ways the so-called Western religions, Judaism, Christianity and Islam; certainly in terms of language and myth their general connection to European cultures is clear. Therefore, what is referred to as "Indian religion" is a fertile matrix of cultural materials that has in turn had a pervasive influence upon other specific religious traditions in antiquity, while exerting a direct and continuing influence into the contemporary period. The separate materials have also exercised a deep fascination for members of modern society. Since the European Romantics discovered the East, numerous intellectuals have been drawn to the ideas and practices of India as a rich lode of religious lore and practice; such ideas apparently provide an alternative to the more rational and reductive religious aspects of European cultures. Of course both scholars and practitioners of religion have experienced this attraction; it is the resources developed by the former group that will be briefly noted here.

India certainly represents an original fount of religion, one that influenced both East and West. But, in another sense, the religious materials of this culture are only so identified as a result of Western imperialism. Even the term "Hinduism," understood as designating a particular religion, is a conceptualization precipitated out of cultural contact in the eighteenth century. It is, so to speak, the naming of cultural materials so that they would be intelligible to Westerners. In this particular sense, Hinduism as a religion is the creation, figuratively, of the British East India Company—or, in a more neutral phrase, it is an outcome of cultural interaction between Europeans and India under the conditions set by Western imperialism. A compilation of relevant materials by Peter J. Marshall in *The British Discovery of Hinduism in the Eighteenth Century* (1970) provides a means to see this process at work. For a presentation of Indian religion in its cultural setting, consult A. L. Basham, *The Wonder That Was India* (1954). Louis Dumont discusses the relationship between religion and the Indian social structure in *Homo Hierarchicus: The Caste System and Its Implications* (1966).

There are general presentations of Hinduism, written by Hindu authors, for Western readers. Examples of recent publications of this type are Dittakavi Subrahmanya Sarma, *Essence of Hinduism* (1971), Satischandra Chatterjee, *The Fundamentals of Hinduism* (1970), and T. M. P. Mahadevan, *Outlines of Hinduism* (1956). Kenneth Morgan, an American scholar, edited a variant of this literature; his compilation of essays on different aspects of Hinduism by leading Indian scholars is titled *The Religion of the Hindus* (1953).

Western scholars who have undertaken to study Hinduism have been less concerned to portray it as a fabric of teachings, rituals, writings, etc. Emphasis in this literature typically falls on historical questions, such as those entailed in the development of particular schools and the relations between them. Louis Renou, *The Nature of Hinduism* (1963), is a standard account supplemented by an anthology he edited with introductions. Other introductory studies include T. J. Hopkins, *The Hindu Religious Tradition* (1971) and Sarasvati Chennakesavan's *A Critical Study of Hinduism* (1974).

Technically, the Indian religious culture, with its emphasis on karma and rebirth, emerged in classical form about 2,600 years ago.

Standing behind it was a period of Vedic religion which, in turn, had displaced an earlier culture in the Indus Valley. In broad terms, the classical Hindu pattern included different ways of, or patterns for, life. The way of action, or karma, in central respects carried on Vedic practices. In its early stages this complex of activities included both public sacrifices (which related to the worship of images) and domestic rites (connected with personal and family life). The latter continued as the center of this way for which the Brahmans provided religious leadership. More strictly popular rituals, which continue in contemporary village life, have also been assimilated into this strand of Hinduism. Characteristically, the way of action (or karmic path) entailed duties or prescribed patterns of behavior in terms of the caste and class divisions in Indian society. The existence of these norms within the Hindu tradition has led to discussion of Hindu ethics in Western literature (noted below).

The way of mystical knowledge is a second pattern within classical Hinduism. This is nonritualistic, as the term implies, and does not involve the Brahman caste as religious leaders. The literary deposit of this strand of Hinduism is the *Upanishads,* selections of which are available in various editions. Religious practice of this way led to an extremely refined tradition of meditation—Yoga—and entailed a withdrawal from the world of action. A standard discussion is Mircea Eliade, *Yoga: Immortality and Freedom* (1958). This aspect of Hinduism has stimulated interest among Westerners with its parallels to monastic practices in the West and its legendary holy figures. Of course, Yoga has held a special fascination for the recent West, which is noted later in this section. There are also broad parallels in the philosophical elaboration of religious issues between this strand of Indian culture and aspects of Western religious thought.

The third strand of classical Hinduism is the way of devotion, or bhakti. Among the major cults, one is dedicated to the worship of Rama, a second is the Krishna cult, and the third is Siva worship. A parallel version, Saktism, devoted to feminine deities, stands behind esoteric Tantrism, which is also a subject of current interest.

These short paragraphs have delineated central aspects of the religiously rich Indian culture that became interpreted as Hinduism at the point of its penetration by aggressive Western culture. It is not surprising that modern forms of Hinduism should have rapidly evolved from this interaction. For an overview of this development, see D. S. Sarma, *The Renaissance of Hinduism* (1944), which suggests the plasticity of the recent period. The most prominent movement dedicated to the revitalization of Hindu mysticism was led by Sri Ramakrishna, about whom there are several biographies by followers. Swāmī Vivekānanda extended the Ramakrishna movement overseas, particularly to the United States. Inseparable from other responses to the modern world has been the assertion of religious nationalism in several forms. In these developments, the comingling of traditional, Western, and political ideals is so thorough that the designation Hindu is rendered problematical.

Recent scholarship has attended to numerous and specific topics and figures within the extensive reaches of the tradition so sketched. For the purposes of this guide it may be most useful to indicate some of the more particular kinds of studies undertaken. First, the issue of normative behavior has received attention. As indicated above, it is directly related to the way of action or the Brahman strand of Hinduism. Among recent publications, Shrinivas G. Sathage has written on *Moral Choice and Early Hindu Thought* (1970). A study by S. Cromwell Crawford is concerned with *The Evolution of Hindu Ethical Ideals* (1974). See also Surinder Mohan Bhardwaj's *Hindu Places of Pilgrimage in India: A Study in Cultural Geography* (1973). There has also been considerable interest in the mystical stream in Hinduism. See, for example, Mahendranath Sircar, *Hindu Mysticism According to the Upaniṣads* (1974). David M. Miller's studies have culminated in *Hindu Monastic Life: The Monks and Monasteries of Bhubaneswar* (1976).

In a comparative vein, see several works by distinguished Western scholars: Robert C. Zaehner, *Hindu and Muslim Mysticism* (1960); and Ninian Smart, *The Yogi and the Devotee: The Inter Play between the Upanishads and Catholic Theology* (1968). On the conceptual side, recent works include Troy W. Organ, *The Hindu Quest for the Perfection of Man* (1970) and Floyd H. Ross, *The Meaning of Life in Hinduism and Buddhism* (1952). Also see Susan Snow Wadley, *Shakti: Power in the Conceptual Structure of Karimpur Religion* (1975).

Religious aspects of modern Indian culture have been studied in a variety of frameworks. For a broadly Freudian approach, see Philip Spratt, *Hindu Culture and Personality: A Psycho-analytic Study* (1966). Erik Erikson's *Ghandi's Truth on the Origins of Militant Nonviolence* (1969) is more narrowly focused and informed by ego-psychology. A general summary review of the moral resources in this spiritual civilization is Creighton Lacy's *The Conscience of India: Moral Traditions in the Modern World* (1965). Milton B. Singer, *When a Great Tradition Modernizes: An Anthropological Approach to Indian Civilization* (1972) is more directly concerned with the cultural framework. For a recent analysis of the direct effects on traditional religions of the modern era, see Philip H. Ashby, *Modern Trends in Hinduism* (1974), as well as Lawrence A. Babb's *The Divine Hierarchy: Popular Hinduism in Central India* (1975).

The above paragraphs indicate the extraordinary scope of the high religious life of the Indian subcontinent, the complexity of the issues involved in study of it, and the range of recent literature concerned with it. The concluding paragraphs will identify a few additional resources with concern for two issues: (1) current directions in scholarship about the religious aspects of the broader tradition, and (2) the particular literature focused upon the interaction between Hinduism and the West, or the scholarly (as opposed to popular) presentation of Indian ideas in Western circles.

Ainslie T. Embree edited a useful introduction in *The Hindu Tradition* (1966). On the issue of gods, see Edward Moor, *The Hindu Pantheon* (1968) and Alain Daniélou, *Hindu Polytheism* (1964). Thomas M. Berry, *Religions of India: Hinduism, Yoga, Buddhism* (1971) emphasizes the religious pluralism so deeply ingrained in this culture. Two relatively recent surveys may be useful: Herbert H. Stroup, *Like a Great River: An Introduction to Hinduism* (1972), and Robert C. Zaehner's brief comprehensive introduction, *Hindusm* (1962). Bardwell Smith, editor of *Hinduism: New Essays in the History of Religions* (1976), suggests the kinds of scholarship currently under way in the West, while Kashi Nath Upadhyaya, *Early Buddhism and the Bhagavad-gītā* (1971) and Raj Bali Pandey, *Hindu Samskāras: Socio-religious Study of the Hindu Sacraments* (1969) suggest directions in scholarship among Indian scholars.

Finally, Raymond Panikkar, *The Vedic Experience: Mantramanjarī: An Anthology of the Vedas for Modern Man and Contemporary Celebration* (1977), indicates the scholarly level of current interest in relations between Indian traditions and the West. See also Panikkar's *The Unknown Christ of Hinduism* (1964). Nand K. Devaraja, *Hinduism and Christianity* (1969) and Kavalam M. Panikkar, *Hinduism and the West: A Study in Challenge and Response* (1964) also indicate the continued vitality of the rich traditions.

By design, this guide is giving only secondary attention to scholarship on Eastern religion. The above paragraphs are intended to suggest the centrality of Indian religious materials, their inherent richness and complexity, and the range of current scholarship on Hinduism and related phenomena; they are not intended to be a bibliographical resource for specialized research.

Ashby, Philip H. *Modern Trends in Hinduism.* New York: Columbia Univ. Pr., 1974.

Babb, Lawrence A. *The Divine Hierarchy: Popular Hinduism in Central India.* New York: Columbia Univ. Pr., 1975.

Basham, A. L. *The Wonder That Was India: A Survey of the Culture of the Indian Subcontinent before the Coming of the Muslims.* London: Sidgwick, 1954.

Berry, Thomas M. *Religions of India: Hinduism, Yoga, Buddhism.* New York: Bruce, 1971.

Bhardwaj, Surinder Mohan. *Hindu Places of Pilgrimage in India: A Study in Cultural Geography.* Berkeley: Univ. of California Pr., 1973.

Brown, W. Norman. *Man in the Universe: Some Cultural Continuities in India.* Berkeley: Univ. of California Pr., 1970.

Chatterjee, Satischandra. *The Fundamentals of Hinduism.* Calcutta: Univ. of Calcutta, 1970.

Chennakesavan, Sarasvati. *A Critical Study of Hinduism.* New York: Asia Pub. House, 1974.

Crawford, S. Cromwell. *The Evolution of Hindu Ethical Ideals.* Calcutta: Firma K. L. Mukhopadhyay, 1974.

Daniélou, Alain. *Hindu Polytheism.* New York: Pantheon, 1964.

Devaraja, Nand K. *Hinduism and Christianity.* New York: Asia Pub. House, 1969.

Dumont, Louis. *Homo Hierarchicus: The Caste System and Its Implications.* Chicago: Univ. of Chicago Pr., 1966.

Eliade, Mircea. *Yoga: Immortality and Freedom.* Tr. by W. R. Trask. New York: Pantheon, 1958.

Embree, Ainslie T., ed. *The Hindu Tradition.* New York: Modern Library, 1966.

Erikson, Erik. *Ghandi's Truth on the Origins of Militant Nonviolence.* New York: Norton, 1969.

Hopkins, T. J. *The Hindu Religious Tradition.* Encino, Calif.: Dickenson, 1971.

Lacy, Creighton. *The Conscience of India: Moral Traditions in the Modern World.* New York: Holt, Rinehart & Winston, 1965.

Mahadevan, T. M. P. *Outlines of Hinduism.* Bombay: Chetana, 1956.

Marshall, Peter J. *The British Discovery of Hinduism in the Eighteenth Century.* Cambridge: Cambridge Univ. Pr., 1970.

Miller, David M. *Hindu Monastic Life: The Monks and Monasteries of Bhubaneswar.* Montreal: McGill-Queen's Univ. Pr., 1976.

Moor, Edward. *The Hindu Pantheon.* Varanasi: Indological Book House, 1968.

Morgan, Kenneth. *The Religion of the Hindus.* New York: Ronald, 1953.

Organ, Troy W. *The Hindu Quest for the Perfection of Man.* Athens: Ohio Univ. Pr., 1970.

Pandey, Raj Bali. *Hindu Samskāras: Socio-religious Study of the Hindu Sacraments.* Delhi: Motilal Banarsidass, 1969.

Panikkar, Kavalam M. *Hinduism and the West: A Study in Challenge and Response.* Chandigarth: Panjab Univ. Pub. Bureau, 1964.

Panikkar, Raymond. *The Unknown Christ of Hinduism.* London: Darton, 1964.

————. *The Vedic Experience: Mantramanjari: An Anthology of the Vedas for Modern Man and Contemporary Celebration.* Berkeley: Univ. of California Pr., 1977.

Renou, Louis. *The Nature of Hinduism.* Tr. by Patrick Evans. New York: Walker, 1963.

————, ed. *Hinduism.* New York: Braziller, 1961.

Ross, Floyd H. *The Meaning of Life in Hinduism and Buddhism.* London: Routledge, 1952.

Sarma, Dittakavi Subrahmanya. *Essence of Hinduism.* Bombay: Bharatiya Vidya Bhavan, 1971.

————. *The Renaissance of Hinduism.* Varanasi: Hindu Univ. Pr., 1944.

Sathage, Shrinivas G. *Moral Choice and Early Hindu Thought.* Bombay: Jaico Pub. House, 1970.

Singer, Milton B. *When a Great Tradition Modernizes: An Anthropological Approach to Indian Civilization.* New York: Praeger, 1972.

Sircar, Mahendranath. *Hindu Mysticism According to the Upaniṣads.* (1934.) Repr.: New Delhi: Oriental Books Repr. Corp., 1974.

Smart, Ninian. *The Yogi and the Devotee: The Inter Play between the Upanishads and Catholic Theology.* London: Allen & Unwin, 1968.

Smith, Bardwell, ed. *Hinduism: New Essays in the History of Religions.* Leiden: Brill, 1976.

Spratt, Philip. *Hindu Culture and Personality: A Psycho-analytic Study.* Bombay: Manaktalas, 1966.

Stroup, Herbert H. *Like a Great River: An Introduction to Hinduism.* New York: Harper & Row, 1972.

Upadhyaya, Kashi Nath. *Early Buddhism and the Bhagavad-gītā.* Delhi: Motilal Banarsidass, 1971.

Wadley, Susan Snow. *Shakti: Power in the Conceptual Structure of Karimpur Religion.* Chicago: Univ. of Chicago Pr., 1975.

Zaehner, Robert C. *Hindu and Muslim Mysticism.* London: Univ. of London, Athlone Pr., 1960.

————. *Hinduism.* London: Home Univ. Lib., 1962.

BUDDHISM

Buddhism seems to represent to modern historians a religious tradition more directly comparable to Judaism and Christianity than Hinduism, and thus, perhaps, more readily intelligible. It was begun at a point in time by a venerated figure; it possesses teachings that have been applied and elaborated through millennia; it has developed in distinctive ways in relationship to widely divergent societies; it has demonstrated a strong ascetic impulse; and has divided into separate schools or groups reminiscent of the marked subtraditions of Western religions. But in other respects broad comparisons fail. The Buddha remains a thoroughly elusive historical figure whose identity and significance is not so determined by a prior tradition as, for instance, Moses for Judaism or Jesus for Christianity; the teachings seem systematically elusive to Westerners; while this world is transitory in Buddhism, there is not a supernatural God or a collective salvation. This elusive possibility of comparison, and the difficulties inherent in making precise comparisons, has contributed to the remarkable recent interest in Buddhism on the part of Western scholars of religions.

Much current scholarly interest in Buddhism also rises from the extraordinary increase in Southeast Asian and East Asian area studies in American universities. As these regions have become subjects of interest because of their geopolitical importance and in terms of their cultural characteristics (for reasons that relate directly to the role of the United States as a world power), their histories, languages, literatures, politics, and behavioral patterns generally—in short their cultures—have been intensively studied. The net result of this veritable explosion of Western interest has been to enhance possibilities for the study of Buddhism. On this question, see Peter A. Pardue, *Buddhism: A Historical Introduction to Buddhist Values and the Social and Political Forms They Have Assumed in Asia* (1971). But, at the same time, that objective has appeared less sharply focused due to the manifoldness of the tradition; its internal complexity has seemed overwhelming. (This is a close parallel, not surprisingly, to a recently enhanced appreciation for the importance of Christianity within Western cultural history simultaneous to a recognition of its internal pluralism and high degree of particularity.) These perspectives introduce brief comments on scholarship with respect to Buddhism. In this short guide emphasis will be given to specifically religious questions although, under the circumstances described, no strict separation between these and other cultural dimensions of East Asian societies is possible.

The Buddha, or Enlightened One, was born in India as Siddhartha Gautama and, by tradition, lived a full life of eighty years. While there is disagreement about the precise dates, there is general consensus (based upon various traditional and critical positions) that the bulk of his life fell in the sixth century before the common era by Western dating. For particulars of the issues entailed, see the translated version of Foucher's *The Life of the Buddha, According to the Ancient Texts and Monuments of India* (1963). Another discussion is available in E. J. Thomas, *The Life of Buddha as Legend and History* (1949). In addition to their historical quest for the Buddha, Westerners have also had a literary interest in his life, resulting in a number of fictional representations. Traditional accounts of the Buddha are given in both Pali texts and biographies written in Sanskrit. Of course Buddhahood is the goal of all—and held to be achieved by many others as well—so that exemplary Buddhists are also well remembered and idealized in the separate national traditions.

The second essential of Buddhism is doctrine, which roots in several groups of canonical texts. One set consists of the rules of discipline. Another set is the teachings actually attributed to Buddha. A third set is the commentaries on the former. These materials are available in the Pali Canon that stands behind the Theravada tradition of Buddhism in Southeast Asian cultures. They are also available in Sanskrit versions and as such enter the Mahayana movement of Central and East Asian lands. Technical discussions of the languages involved, and the interrelationships between these schools, movements, or traditions cannot be points of this cursory review. It is important to stress, however, that although these texts have been anthologized for Western readers, they do not form a "Bible" comparable, for example, to the Western Christian scriptures as the codification of revelation and norms of behavior. Rather, Buddhist texts suggest the stance of inquiry through teaching.

The teachings of Buddhism are made real in the life of the Buddha's followers as principles and practices. Western scholars have given specialized attention to its concepts and doctrines, as well as its logic and epistemology and the psychological and ethical aspects of the tradition, among others. But the central thrust of Buddhism as practice is in terms of the goal of enlightenment. In the achievement of enlightenment, conduct, thought, and understanding cohere. *Nirvana* is the outcome sought, an end facilitated through instruction, environment or discipline, and practice. Thus meditation is the basic mode of approach to enlightenment. See Edward Conze, *Buddhist Meditation* (1956) for a general discussion, recognizing that great variations exist in the different Buddhist schools and separate cultural traditions. From this point of view, ritual practices and ceremonies, as important elements of the religion, point back to the central impulse toward meditation.

Finally, Buddhism has been identified with particular kinds of institutions. The Buddhist community is explicitly realized in monastic orders which, again, have assumed different forms in separate cultures. Further, Buddhism has characteristically been represented by a multitude of schools—in some way comparable to the sectarian de-

velopments so endemic to Western Christianity. The arts and literature have also been vehicles for presentation of Buddhism, no less
than the ritual aspects of sacred space.

Comments about whether the Buddha was a historical figure suggest how important cultural and historical perspectives have been in
Western scholarly approaches to Buddhism. A relevant study is Guy
R. Welbon, *The Buddhist Nirvana and Its Western Interpreters*
(1968). A recent important critical discussion by Frank Reynolds of
the first half millennium of Buddhism is available as "The Two
Wheels of Dharma" (see *The Two Wheels of Dharma,* edited by
Bardwell Smith [1972]). Early Buddhism is also discussed by Sukumar Dutt in *The Buddha and the Five After-Centuries* (1957). For an
essay on the changing concepts of the Buddha, see "The Superhuman
Personality of the Buddha" by Andre Bareau (in Kitagawa and Long,
1969).

Western authorities on Buddhism have produced a large literature.
Its range of general interest in the subject is suggested by the following, among many other, volumes. Edward Conze's numerous studies
include *Buddhist Thought in India: Three Phases of Buddhist Philosophy* (1962) that attends to its philosophical dimension. His *Further Buddhist Studies: Selected Essays* (1975), by contrast, is a selection of pieces—essays, articles, and reviews—that suggests both the
complexities encountered in studying Buddhism and its distance from
modern Western perspectives. *Buddhism: A Non-Theistic Religion*
(1970) is the translation of a study (originally in German) by Helmuth von Glasenapp. It is focused on the question of the sense in
which Buddhism is properly (or improperly) identified as a religion.
Richard H. Robinson and Willard L. Johnson's introduction *The
Buddhist Religion: A Historical Introduction* (1970) has had wide
use in academic contexts. Winston L. King has explored the characteristics of Buddhist ethics in the southern tradition in his *In the
Hope of Nibbana: An Essay on Theravada Buddhist Ethics* (1964).

Other studies have embodied, in different ways, a more specifically
comparative intent. Relatively recent efforts of this sort, with emphasis indicated by titles, include Winston L. King, *Buddhism and Christianity: Some Bridges of Understanding* (1962); Heinrich Dumoulin,
Christianity Meets Buddhism (1973); George Appleton, *On the
Eightfold Path: Christian Presence amid Buddhism* (1961); and Michael Pye and Robert Morgan, editors, *The Cardinal Meaning, Essays in Comparative Hermeneutics: Buddhism and Christianity*
(1973). An older study by B. H. Streeter, *The Buddha and the Christ*

(1933), remains useful. A comparative perspective on relations of Buddhism with Hinduism is found in Jamshed Fozdar, *The God of Buddha* (1973).

For reasons indicated in the early paragraphs of this section, the recent study of Buddhism is primarily marked by attention to regional developments. While a comprehensive review is out of the question and would serve no purpose in this context, it is important to indicate some things about the distribution of this literature.

Historically, of course, Buddhism was linked to sources in the Indian subcontinent. A general introduction to its place in the region of origin is Trevor O. Ling, *The Buddha: Buddhist Civilization in India and Ceylon* (1973). With respect to contemporary Burma, Melford Spiro, an anthropologist, has offered a comprehensive analysis of the tradition in his *Buddhism and Society: A Great Tradition and Its Burmese Vicissitudes* (1970). His earlier *Burmese Supernaturalism: A Study in the Explanation and Reduction of Suffering* (1967) was concerned with complementary folk religion in the same culture. A close-order description and discussion of Burmese worship practices is provided in a slight volume by T. U. Pe Maung, *Buddhist Devotion and Dedication* (1964). A more philosophically oriented discussion of the Burmese tradition is Robert H. L. Slater, *Paradox and Nirvana: A Study of Religious Ultimates with Special Reference to Burmese Buddhism* (1951).

Comparably culture-specific studies are also available for Ceylon. Hans-Dieter Evers, *Monks, Priests and Peasants: A Study of Buddhism and Social Structure in Central Ceylon* (1972) develops a broad discussion of the tradition in that culture on the basis of analysis of a central temple and its relationship to the society. *Precept and Practice: Traditional Buddhism in the Rural Highlands of Ceylon* (1971) by Richard F. Gombrich uses Ceylonese materials as a case study in religious change, but in the process effectively illuminates Buddhism in that setting.

The place of Buddhism in Thai society has also received attention from anthropologists. A comprehensive study is Stanley J. Tambiah, *World Conqueror and World Renouncer: A Study of Buddhism and Polity in Thailand against a Historical Background* (1976). Although focused in the present, it locates Thai Buddhism in relationship to its development from Indian sources. A prior study by the same author, *Buddhism and Spirit Cults in Northeastern Thailand* (1970), is developed from the point of view of peasant and village life. Jane Bunnag's *Buddhist Monk, Buddhist Layman: A Study of Urban Monastic Or-*

ganization in Central Thailand (1973) concerns the complementary urban and monastic materials.

Buddhism entered China at approximately the beginning of the Christian era in the West. Broadly speaking, once there the Mahayana tradition developed into a number of new schools that took different directions. The basic studies cited below indicate the major lines of development. General discussions of these episodes may be found in Arthur F. Wright, *Buddhism in Chinese History* (1959), Kenneth K. S. Chen, *The Chinese Transformation of Buddhism* (1973) and *Buddhism in China* (1964). It is generally held that, after prolonged persecutions in the ninth century, Buddhism never recovered the place in Chinese life it had earlier achieved. A recent monograph calls attention to popular forms of Buddhism: Daniel Overmyer, *Folk Buddhist Religion: Dissenting Sects in Late Traditional China* (1976). Buddhism in recent China has been the subject of work by Holmes Welch. See his three volumes: *The Practice of Chinese Buddhism: 1900–1950* (1967); *The Buddhist Revival in China* (1968); and *Buddhism under Mao* (1972). See also Wing-tsit Chan, *Religious Trends in Modern China* (1953).

It has been conventional to view China as a fundamentally secular society that absorbed and contained the Buddhist tradition, thus managing to minimize its influence upon the basic culture. Recent scholarship certainly questions the latter half of the position, and the premise, or former half, is also currently under challenge. On these issues, see the brief section on religions of China discussed later in the essay.

Certainly Buddhism has been very important as a religious tradition in Japan. A popular treatment is E. Dale Saunders's *Buddhism in Japan, with an Outline of Its Origins in India* (1964). An older study by August Karl Reischauer continues to be useful and has been reprinted: *Studies in Japanese Buddhism* (1917). Particular schools of Buddhism have also been treated. See, for example, Heinrich Dumoulin, *A History of Zen Buddhism* (1963). Also, the writings of D. T. Suzuki, such as *Zen and Japanese Culture* (1970), directly discuss this subject.

In the case of Buddhism a tradition of critical Japanese scholarship has developed that complements Western analysis of the subject. A periodical, *The Eastern Buddhist,* published in Kyoto by the Eastern Buddhist Society at Otani University, regularly prints useful articles on Buddhism in Japan. See also such books as Shōkō Watanabe, *Japanese Buddhism: A Critical Appraisal* (1968) and Shinshō Hanayama, *A History of Japanese Buddhism* (1960).

As a result of the political changes in Tibet in the 1950s, culminating in the flight of the Dalai Lama in 1959, numerous studies of this culture have been undertaken, including special attention to Tibetan Buddhism. For a general introduction, see Hugh Richardson and David Snellgrove, *A Cultural History of Tibet* (1968), as well as Helmut Hoffmann, *The Religions of Tibet* (1961). For a review of traditional materials that underlie modern scholarship, see A. I. Vostrikov, *Tibetan Historical Literature* (1970), and Giuseppe Tucci, "The Validity of Tibetan Historical Traditions" (in Bosch, 1947).

With respect to philosophical schools and mystical practices, see John Blofeld, *The Tantric Mysticism of Tibet* (1970). The same author has also published *The Way of Power: A Practical Guide to the Tantric Mysticism of Tibet* (1970). Alex Wayman, *The Buddhist Tantras: Light on Indo-Tibetan Esotericism* (1973) is important. Herbert Guenther has undertaken to interpret Vajrayana thought in a number of studies. Among them see *The Tantric View of Life* (1969), and *Buddhist Philosophy in Theory and Practice* (1972). Ritual expressions of Tibetan Buddhism are presented in Robert Ekvall, *Religious Observances in Tibet: Patterns and Function* (1964). Also see Sherry B. Ortner, *Sherpas through Their Rituals* (1978). These few references suggest the depth of current Western scholarly interest in Tibetan materials. The cultural consequence of the Chinese imperialism has been to displace and fundamentally threaten continuation of ancient traditions.

These few paragraphs and citations can do no more than suggest the richness of the Buddhist tradition and the current lines of scholarly study directed to it. What should be clear is that the powerful impulse to critical historical analysis of religious traditions in the East—as in the West—derives from the Western Enlightenment, rather than that promised in the Buddhist tradition. In this sense, when a self-sustaining Eastern tradition of modern scholarship has emerged, as in Japan, the impulse for that too has been stimulated from the same Western sources, although the lines of its development have been unique.

Appleton, George. *On the Eightfold Path: Christian Presence amid Buddhism.* New York: Oxford Univ. Pr., 1961.
Bareau, Andre. "The Superhuman Personality of the Buddha." In *Myths and Symbols,* ed. by Kitagawa and Long. Chicago: Univ. of Chicago Pr., 1969
Blofeld, John. *The Tantric Mysticism of Tibet: A Practical Guide.* New York: Dutton, 1970.

————. *The Way of Power: A Practical Guide to the Tantric Mysticism of Tibet*. London: Allen & Unwin, 1970.

Bunnag, Jane. *Buddhist Monk, Buddhist Layman: A Study of Urban Monastic Organization in Central Thailand*. Cambridge: Cambridge Univ. Pr., 1973.

Burtt, E. A., ed. *The Teachings of the Compassionate Buddha*. New York: New American Library, 1955.

Chan, Wing-tsit. *Religious Trends in Modern China*. New York: Columbia Univ. Pr., 1953.

Chen, Kenneth K. S. *Buddhism in China*. Princeton, N.J.: Princeton Univ. Pr., 1964.

————. *The Chinese Transformation of Buddhism*. Princeton, N.J.: Princeton Univ. Pr., 1973.

Conze, Edward. *Buddhist Meditation*. London: Allen, 1956.

————. *Buddhist Thought in India: Three Phases of Buddhist Philosophy*. London: Allen, 1962.

————. *Further Buddhist Studies: Selected Essays*. Oxford: B. Cassirer, 1975.

Dumoulin, Heinrich. *Christianity Meets Buddhism*. Tr. by J. C. Maraldo. Chicago: Open Court, 1973.

————. *A History of Zen Buddhism*. Tr. by Paul Peachey. New York: Pantheon Books, 1963.

Dutt, Sukumar. *The Buddha and the Five After-Centuries*. London: Luzac, 1957.

Ekvall, Robert. *Religious Observances in Tibet: Patterns and Function*. Chicago: Univ. of Chicago Pr., 1964.

Evers, Hans-Dieter. *Monks, Priests and Peasants: A Study of Buddhism and Social Structure in Central Ceylon*. Leiden: Brill, 1972.

Foucher, A. *The Life of the Buddha, According to the Ancient Texts and Monuments of India*. Tr. and abridged by S. B. Boas. Middletown, Conn.: Wesleyan Univ. Pr., 1963.

Fozdar, Jamshed. *The God of Buddha*. New York: Asia Pub. House, 1973.

Glasenapp, Helmuth von. *Buddhism: A Non-Theistic Religion*. New York: Braziller, 1970.

Gombrich, Richard F. *Precept and Practice: Traditional Buddhism in the Rural Highlands of Ceylon*. Oxford: Clarendon Pr., 1971.

Guenther, Herbert. *Buddhist Philosophy in Theory and Practice*. Baltimore: Penguin, 1972.

————. *The Tantric View of Life*. Berkeley, Calif.: Shambhala, 1969.

Hanayama, Shinshō. *A History of Japanese Buddhism*. Tr. and ed. by Kosho Yamamoto. Tokyo: CIIB, 1960.

Hoffmann, Helmut. *The Religions of Tibet*. Tr. by Edward Fitzgerald. London: Allen & Unwin, 1961.

King, Winston L. *Buddhism and Christianity: Some Bridges of Understanding*. Philadelphia: Westminster Pr., 1962.

————. *In the Hope of Nibbana: An Essay on Theravada Buddhist Ethics*. LaSalle, Ill.: Open Court, 1964.

Ling, Trevor O. *The Buddha: Buddhist Civilization in India and Ceylon*. New York: Scribner's, 1973.

Ortner, Sherry B. *Sherpas through Their Rituals.* Cambridge: Cambridge Univ. Pr., 1978.

Overmyer, Daniel. *Folk Buddhist Religion: Dissenting Sects in Late Traditional China.* Cambridge, Mass.: Harvard Univ. Pr., 1976.

Pardue, Peter A. *Buddhism: A Historical Introduction to Buddhist Values and the Social and Political Forms They Have Assumed in Asia.* New York: Macmillan, 1971.

Pe Maung, T. U. *Buddhist Devotion and Dedication.* London: S.P.C.K., 1964.

Pye, Michael, and Robert Morgan, eds. *The Cardinal Meaning, Essays in Comparative Hermeneutics: Buddhism and Christianity.* The Hague: Mouton, 1973.

Reischauer, August Karl. *Studies in Japanese Buddhism.* New York: Macmillan, 1917.

Reynolds, Frank. "The Two Wheels of Dharma." In *The Two Wheels of Dharma,* ed. by Bardwell Smith. Chambersburg, Pa.: AAR, 1972.

Richardson, Hugh, and David Snellgrove. *A Cultural History of Tibet.* London: Weidenfeld & Nicolson, 1968.

Robinson, Richard H., and Willard L. Johnson. *The Buddhist Religion: A Historical Introduction.* Belmont, Calif.: Dickenson, 1970.

Saunders, E. Dale. *Buddhism in Japan, with an Outline of Its Origins in India.* Philadelphia: Univ. of Pennsylvania Pr., 1964.

Slater, Robert H. L. *Paradox and Nirvana: A Study of Religious Ultimates with Special Reference to Burmese Buddhism.* Chicago: Univ. of Chicago Pr., 1951.

Smith, Bardwell, ed. *The Two Wheels of Dharma.* Chambersburg, Pa.: AAR, 1972.

Spiro, Melford. *Buddhism and Society: A Great Tradition and Its Burmese Vicissitudes.* New York: Harper & Row, 1970.

———. *Burmese Supernaturalism: A Study in the Explanation and Reduction of Suffering.* Englewood Cliffs, N.J.: Prentice-Hall, 1967.

Streeter, B. H. *The Buddha and the Christ.* New York: Macmillan, 1933.

Suzuki, D. T. *Zen and Japanese Culture.* Princeton, N.J.: Princeton Univ. Pr., 1970.

Tambiah, Stanley J. *Buddhism and Spirit Cults in Northeastern Thailand.* Cambridge: Cambridge Univ. Pr., 1970.

———. *World Conquerer and World Renouncer: A Study of Buddhism and Polity in Thailand against a Historical Background.* Cambridge: Cambridge Univ. Pr., 1976.

Thomas, Edgar J. *The Life of Buddha as Legend and History.* 3d rev. ed. London: Routledge & Paul, 1949.

Tucci, Giuseppe. "The Validity of Tibetan Historical Traditions." In F. D. K. Bosch et al., *Indian Antiqua.* Leiden: Brill, 1947.

Vostrikov, A. I. *Tibetan Historical Literature.* Tr. by Harish Cupta. Calcutta: IPP, 1970.

Watanabe, Shōkō. *Japanese Buddhism: A Critical Appraisal.* Tokyo: Kokusai Bunka Shinkokai, 1968.

Wayman, Alex. *The Buddhist Tantras: Light on Indo-Tibetan Esotericism.* New York: S. Weiser, 1973.

Welbon, Guy R. *The Buddhist Nirvana and Its Western Interpreters.* Chicago: Univ. of Chicago Pr., 1968.
Welch, Holmes. *Buddhism under Mao.* Cambridge, Mass.: Harvard Univ. Pr., 1972.
———. *The Buddhist Revival in China.* Cambridge, Mass.: Harvard Univ. Pr., 1968.
———. *The Practice of Chinese Buddhism: 1900–1950.* Cambridge, Mass.: Harvard Univ. Pr., 1967.
Wright, Arthur F. *Buddhism in Chinese History.* Stanford, Calif.: Stanford Univ. Pr., 1959.

RELIGIONS OF CHINA AND JAPAN, EXCLUDING BUDDHISM

In the preceding section on Buddhism, attention was given to its important role in Chinese and Japanese history. As the references suggest, it underwent significant and unique development over long periods in each society. Simultaneously, despite this differentiation of the basic tradition, one that parallels the development of separate versions of Christianity in European societies, sufficient family resemblances remain to warrant attention to Chinese and Japanese Buddhism as part of a transcultural religion. The introduction of Buddhism in each culture, however, served as a catalyst with respect to archaic patterns of life and thought. Therefore, brief discussions of the indigenous religious traditions of East Asia are called for here, particularly since modern scholarship has increasingly called attention to them, especially in China and Japan.

In China, the impact of proselytizing religions such as Buddhism (and later Christianity and Islam) upon the indigenous traditions of the society led to development of Taoism and Confucianism as distinctively religious counterparts. At the same time, popular rites and practices, as well as cults associated with public affairs or political regimes, both antedated and continued to have a significant place in the culture. The literature on these religious aspects of China has been increasingly rich. Only brief comments can be offered here.

Confucius lived in the sixth and fifth centuries B.C. (by Western dating) and was the most prominent among numerous teachers or philosophers. A biography is available by H. G. Creel, *Confucius and the Chinese Way* (1960), which is a reprint of *Confucius, the Man and the Myth* (1949). A recent study by Herbert Fingarette has stimulated interest: *Confucius: The Secular as Sacred* (1972). Mencius, Confucius' most prominent successor, lived in the fourth and third centuries before the common era in the West, and worked to dedivinize or secularize his teaching.

With the construction of the Empire at the end of the third century B.C. and the cultural reaction to it, Confucianism emerged as a state cult and, in response to the introduction of Buddhism, Taoism developed as a religious rendering of the Chinese philosophical teachings. See Chung-yuan Chang, *Creativity and Taoism: A Study of Chinese Philosophy, Art and Poetry* (1963); H. Welch, *The Parting of the Way: Lao Tzu and the Taoist Movement* (1957); and M. Kaltenmark, *Lao Tzu and Taoism* (1969). The mystical aspects of Taoism in relationship to the philosophical schools is discussed in Arthur Waley, *Three Ways of Thought in Ancient China* (1946). See also Wing-tsit Chan, *The Way of Lao-tzu* (1963).

Neo-Confucianism developed in the second millennium of the common era in the West, in part as an attempt to revitalize Chinese traditions so as to purge Buddhism from the culture. See William Theodore De Bary, *The Unfolding of Neo-Confucianism* (1975) and *Self and Society in Ming Thought* (1970), and Carsun Chang, *The Development of Neo-Confucian Thought* (1957).

Attention is given to Confucian and Neo-Confucian thought within the broader context of Chinese culture in two sets of essays published in the 1950s. *Studies in Chinese Thought* (1953), edited by Arthur F. Wright, and *Chinese Thought and Institutions* (1957), edited by John K. Fairbank, are valuable collections. See also Arthur F. Wright (editor), *The Confucian Persuasion* (1960). A sustained discussion of the challenge to traditional Confucian attitudes and patterns of thought in modern China is found in J. R. Levenson, *Confucian China and Its Modern Fate* (1958).

Religious developments of the recent past were placed in social and historical perspective in C. K. Yang, *Religion in Chinese Society: A Study of Contemporary Social Functions of Religion and Some of Their Historical Factors* (1961). Analysis of these changes is also given in Wing-tsit Chan, *Religious Trends in Modern China* (1953). The policies adopted by the Peoples Republic are discussed by Donald E. MacInnes in his *Religious Policy and Practice in Communist China* (1972). A very different genre of work is represented in a recent anthropological study of folk religion in Taiwan available in David K. Jordan, *Gods, Ghosts, and Ancestors: The Folk Religion of a Taiwanese Village* (1972).

There is a full literature on specifically religious aspects of historic and modern Japanese culture. An excellent general review is provided by Joseph M. Kitagawa, *Religion in Japanese History* (1966). A more popular introduction is *Japanese Religion: Unity and Diversity* (1969) by H. Byron Earhart. A collection of separate studies by respected Japanese scholars may also hold interest: see *Religious Studies in Japan* (1959), published by the Japanese Association for Religious Studies.

A very general bibliography cannot call attention to specialized questions, such as available resources concerning ancient Japanese religion, including the relation of the Ainu to Japanese traditions. Notice should be taken, however, of Shinto; as the Japanese national cult, it is widely studied and serves as a prominent case in civil religion discussions. An older, thorough monograph is *A Study of Shinto: The Religion of the Japanese Nation* (1926; reprint, 1971) by Genchi Katō. Several additional older studies may also be useful: Daniel C. Holtom, *The National Faith of Japan: A Study of Modern Shinto* (1938; reprint, 1965) and A. C. Underwood, *Shintoism: The Indigenous Religion of Japan* (1934). More recent studies include: Jean Herbert, *Shinto: At the Fountain-Head of Japan* (1967); Montonori Ono, *Shinto: The Kami Way* (1961); and Floyd H. Ross, *Shinto, the Way of Japan* (1965).

Japanese folk religion is analyzed in Ichirō Hori, *Folk Religion in Japan*, edited by J. M. Kitagawa and Alan Miller (1968). See also U. S. Casal, *The Five Sacred Festivals of Ancient Japan: Their Symbolism and Historical Development* (1967), and H. Byron Earhart, *A Religious Study of the Mount Haguro Sect of Shugendō: An Example of Japanese Mountain Religion* (1970). An especially fine study of the folk tradition is Carmen Blacker, *The Catalpa Bow: A Study of Shamanistic Practices in Japan* (1975).

The range of religious developments in the recent centuries has been very significant. As background, Robert Bellah's study, *Tokugawa Religion: The Values of Pre-Industrial Japan* (1957) is written from a broadly Weberian perspective on religion and society. For the succeeding period, see H. Kishimoto (editor), *Japanese Religion in the Meiji Era* (1956). A broad summary review at midcentury is available in William K. Bunce, *Religions in Japan: Buddhism, Shinto, Christianity* (1959).

For the contemporary situation, see *Japanese Religion: A Survey, by the Agency for Cultural Affairs* (1972). Sociological perspectives on Japanese religion are available in Edward Norbeck, *Religion and Society in Modern Japan: Continuity and Change* (1970) and Kiyomi Morioka and William Newell (editors), *The Sociology of Japanese*

Religion (1968), which includes general analysis as well as case studies. For new movements, see H. Neill McFarland, *The Rush Hour of the Gods: A Study of New Religious Movements in Japan* (1967). A bibliography of resources on the many new religions was developed by H. Byron Earhart in his *The New Religions of Japan: A Bibliography of Western-Language Materials* (1970). Finally, Niels C. Nielsen, Jr., has explored the subject of *Religion and Philosophy in Contemporary Japan* (1957).

References have been made in the preceding section on Buddhism to specialized studies of Buddhism in China and Japan.

Bellah, Robert. *Tokugawa Religion: The Values of Pre-Industrial Japan.* Glencoe, Ill.: Free Pr., 1957.

Blacker, Carmen. *The Catalpa Bow: A Study of Shamanistic Practices in Japan.* London: Allen & Unwin, 1975.

Bunce, William K. *Religions in Japan: Buddhism, Shinto, Christianity.* Rutland, Vt.: Tuttle, 1955, 1959.

Casal, U. S. *The Five Sacred Festivals of Ancient Japan: Their Symbolism and Historical Development.* Tokyo: Sophia Univ., 1967.

Chan, Wing-tsit. *Religious Trends in Modern China.* New York: Columbia Univ. Pr., 1953.

————. *The Way of Lao-tzu.* Indianapolis, Ind.: Bobbs-Merrill, 1963.

————, tr. *Reflections on Things at Hand: The Neo-Confucian Anthology.* New York: Columbia Univ. Pr., 1967.

Chang, Carsun. *The Development of Neo-Confucian Thought.* New York: Twayne, 1957.

Chang, Chung-yuan. *Creativity and Taoism: A Study of Chinese Philosophy, Art and Poetry.* New York: Julian Pr., 1963.

Creel, H. G. *Confucius and the Chinese Way.* New York: Harper & Row, 1960. Reprint of *Confucius, the Man and the Myth.* New York: John Day, 1949.

De Bary, William Theodore. *Self and Society in Ming Thought.* New York: Columbia Univ. Pr., 1970.

————. *The Unfolding of Neo-Confucianism.* New York: Columbia Univ. Pr., 1975.

Dobson, W. A. C. H. *Mencius.* Toronto: Univ. of Toronto Pr., 1963.

Earhart, H. Byron. *Japanese Religion: Unity and Diversity.* Belmont, Calif.: Dickenson, 1969.

————. *The New Religions of Japan: A Bibliography of Western-Language Materials.* Tokyo: Sophia Univ., 1970.

————. *A Religious Study of the Mount Haguro Sect of Shugendō: An Example of Japanese Mountain Religion.* Tokyo: Sophia Univ., 1970.

Fairbank, John K., ed. *Chinese Thought and Institutions.* Chicago: Univ. of Chicago Pr., 1957.

Fingarette, Herbert. *Confucius: The Secular as Sacred.* New York: Harper & Row, 1972.

Herbert, Jean. *Shintō: At the Fountain-Head of Japan.* London: Allen & Unwin, 1967.

Holtom, Daniel C. *The National Faith of Japan: A Study of Modern Shinto.* New York: Dutton, 1938, 1965.

Hori, Ichirō. *Folk Religion in Japan.* Ed. by J. M. Kitagawa and Alan Miller. Chicago: Univ. of Chicago Pr., 1968.

Japanese Association for Religious Studies. *Religious Studies in Japan.* Tokyo: Maruzen, 1959.

Japanese Religion: A Survey, by the Agency for Cultural Affairs. Tokyo: Kodansha International, 1972.

Jordan, David K. *Gods, Ghosts, and Ancestors: The Folk Religion of a Taiwanese Village.* Berkeley: Univ. of California Pr., 1972.

Kaltenmark, M. *Lao Tzu and Taoism.* Tr. by Roger Greaves. Stanford, Calif.: Stanford Univ. Pr., 1969.

Katō, Genchi. *A Study of Shinto: The Religion of the Japanese Nation.* Tokyo: Meiji Japan Society, 1926, 1971.

Kishimoto, H., ed. *Japanese Religion in the Meiji Era.* Tr. and adapted by J. F. Howes. Tokyo: Obunsha, 1956.

Kitagawa, Joseph M. *Religion in Japanese History.* New York: Columbia Univ. Pr., 1966.

Levenson, J. R. *Confucian China and Its Modern Fate.* Berkeley: Univ. of California Pr., 1958.

MacInnes, Donald E. *Religious Policy and Practice in Communist China.* New York: Macmillan, 1972.

McFarland, H. Neill. *The Rush Hour of the Gods: A Study of New Religious Movements in Japan.* New York: Macmillan, 1967.

Morioka, Kiyomi, and William Newell, eds. *The Sociology of Japanese Religion.* Leiden: Brill, 1968.

Nielsen, Niels C., Jr. *Religion and Philosophy in Contemporary Japan.* Houston: Rice Institute, 1957.

Norbeck, Edward. *Religion and Society in Modern Japan: Continuity and Change.* Houston: Rice University, 1970.

Ono, Montonori. *Shinto: The Kami Way.* Rutland, Vt.: Bridgeway Pr., 1961.

Ross, Floyd H. *Shinto, the Way of Japan.* Boston: Beacon Pr., 1965.

Underwood, A. C. *Shintoism: The Indigenous Religion of Japan.* London: Epworth, 1934.

Waley, Arthur. *Three Ways of Thought in Ancient China.* London: Allen & Unwin, 1946.

Welch, H. *The Parting of the Way: Lao Tzu and the Taoist Movement.* Boston: Beacon Pr., 1957.

Wright, A. F., ed. *The Confucian Persuasion.* Stanford, Calif.: Stanford Univ. Pr., 1960.

——, ed. *Studies in Chinese Thought.* Chicago: Univ. of Chicago Pr., 1953.

Yang, C. K. *Religion in Chinese Society: A Study of Contemporary Social Functions of Religion and Some of Their Historical Factors.* Berkeley: Univ. of California Pr., 1961.

RELIGION IN NEAR EASTERN ANTIQUITY AND THE CLASSICAL WORLD

The ancient Near East and the classical world of Greece and Rome formed the matrix for the great Western religions, Judaism, Christianity and, subsequently, Islam. A distinguished body of scholarship has developed on the many religious aspects of this turbulent and dynamic region in early historic eras. This section will briefly review resources available for further study, emphasizing those facets that have yielded the most interesting scholarly studies.

At the outset, some general introductions are useful. Edwin O. James, *The Ancient Gods: The History and Diffusion of Religion in the Ancient Near East and the Eastern Mediterranean* (1960) is a discussion of central religious issues throughout the region in historic times. Samuel G. F. Brandon's *Creation Legends of the Ancient Near East* (1963) is more narrowly focused upon cosmogonies. The relation of myth to ritual, and thence to social structure, has been a significant focus for scholarly analysis of ancient religion. On this theme, see Samuel H. Hooke (editor), *Myth, Ritual, and Kingship: Essays on the Theory and Practice of Kingship in the Ancient Near East and in Israel* (1958). A collaborative review of ancient myths in all of the great civilizations, including those of the Near East, may be found in Samuel N. Kramer (editor), *Mythologies of the Ancient World* (1961).

More specialized studies of the Near East before the Persian conquest include Helmer Ringgren, *Religions of the Ancient Near East* (1973) and Henri Frankfort, *Kingship and the Gods: A Study of Ancient Near Eastern Religion as the Integration of Society and Nature* (1948). For a discussion of the "mythopoetic" nature of thought before Greek philosophy and Hebrew monotheism liberated humanity for critical thinking, see Henri Frankfort and others, *The Intellectual Adventure of Ancient Man: An Essay on Speculative Thought in the Ancient Near East* (1948), also published in part as *Before Philosophy* (1951).

A brief monograph on religion in Mesopotamia is Samuel H. Hooke, *Babylonian and Assyrian Religion* (1953). The Sumerian background is discussed in Samuel N. Kramer, *Sumerian Mythology: A Study of Spiritual and Literary Achievement in the Third Millennium B.C.* (1961).

Several introductions to ancient Egyptian religion review the subject in relatively brief compass; see Jaroslav Černý, *Ancient Egyptian Religion* (1952) and Henri Frankfort, *Ancient Egyptian Religion: An Interpretation* (1948). More extensive presentations include a thematic discussion by Samuel A. B. Mercer, *The Religion of Ancient Egypt* (1949) and a translation from the German of Siegfried Morenz, *Egyptian Religion* (1973). Egyptian materials have held widespread interest, of course, not only in themselves but as background to the emergence of ancient Israel. A series of essays on this topic is available in *The Bible and the Ancient Near East: Essays in Honor of William Foxwell Albright* (1961), edited by G. Ernest Wright.

A survey of Greek and Roman religions is available in Herbert J. Rose's *Religion in Greece and Rome* (1959), which combines two earlier studies. The Greeks are the subject of the following general discussions: William K. C. Guthrie, *The Greeks and Their Gods* (1962), and the older *Five Stages of Greek Religion* by Gilbert Murray (1951). For more specialized studies of Greek religion, see Martin P. Nilsson, *Greek Popular Religion* (1940) (reissued as *Greek Folk Religion*), and *A History of Greek Religion* (1949).

An older study by Francis M. Cornford, *Greek Religious Thought from Homer to the Age of Alexander* (1923), indicates that religious thought was not as separate from other cultural genres as it may seem at present; indeed the culture was in general far less differentiated than its modern counterparts. More specialized studies include William C. Greene, *Moira: Fate, Good, and Evil in Greek Thought* (1944); Eric R. Dodds, *The Greeks and the Irrational* (1951); and Karl Kerényi, *The Religion of the Greeks and Romans* (1962). Two older, classical studies are Jane E. Harrison, *Prolegomena to the Study of Greek Religion* (1922) and Werner Jaeger, *Paideia: The Ideals of Greek Culture* (1939–44).

A survey of Roman religions is available in Robert M. Ogilvie, *The Romans and Their Gods in the Age of Augustus* (1969). Georges Dumézil's *Archaic Roman Religion, with an Appendix on the Religion of the Etruscans* (1970) is especially important; a discussion of his work by C. Scott Littleton may be found in *The New Comparative Mythology: An Anthropological Assessment of the Theories of Georges Dumézil* (1966).

The Greek and Roman legacies came together in a great Mediterranean civilization that was a vital and variegated cultural region for much of a millennium. For an appreciative review of this culture, see Peter R. L. Brown, *The World of Late Antiquity: From Marcus Aurelius to Muhammad* (1971). Arthur Darby Nock's study, *Conver-*

sion: The Old and the New in Religion from Alexander the Great to Augustine of Hippo (1933), focuses on the interaction that was a consequence of religious pluralism. See the recent survey by John Ferguson, *The Religions of the Roman Empire* (1970).

Religion in classical antiquity has provided subjects for notable specialized studies. A few of them, with topics indicated in their titles, are: Martin P. Nilsson, *The Dionysiac Mysteries of the Hellenistic and Roman Age* (1957); H. Idris Bell, *Cults and Creeds in Graeco-Roman Egypt* (1953); Eve Harris and John R. Harris, *The Oriental Cults in Roman Britain* (1965); Ramsay MacMullen, *Enemies of the Roman Order: Treason, Unrest, and Alienation in the Empire* (1966); Moses Hadas and Morton Smith, *Heroes and Gods: Spiritual Biographies in Antiquity* (1965); André Marie Jean Festugière, *Personal Religion among the Greeks* (1954); Charles N. Cochrane, *Christianity and Classical Culture: A Study of Thought and Action from Augustus to Augustine* (1944); and Eric R. Dodds, *Pagan and Christian in an Age of Anxiety: Some Aspects of Religious Experience from Marcus Aurelius to Constantine* (1965).

Study of Gnosticism has received fresh impetus from the discovery in 1945 of Coptic manuscripts. See Andrew K. Helmbold, *The Nag Hammadi Gnostic Texts and the Bible* (1967). Hans Jonas, *The Gnostic Religion: The Message of the Alien God and the Beginnings of Christianity* (1963) is a brief introduction.

The Zoroastrian tradition, which was the religious expression of the ancient Iranian culture under the Persian Empire, has been widely studied. For an overall interpretation, see Robert C. Zaehner, *The Dawn and Twilight of Zoroastrianism* (1961). Walter B. Henning reviews the founding figure in *Zoroaster: Politician or Witch Doctor?* (1951). Iranian myth and legend is presented in John R. Hinnells, *Persian Mythology* (1973), and Jacques Duchesne-Guillemin analyzes *The Western Response to Zoroaster* (1958). For recent views on Mithraism, an Iranian cult important within the Roman Empire, see John R. Hinnells (editor), *Mithraic Studies* (1973). Specifically on the prophet Mani of the third century of the Christian era, see *Mani and Manichaeism* by Geo Widengren (1965).

Bell, H. Idris. *Cults and Creeds in Graeco-Roman Egypt.* Liverpool: Liverpool Univ. Pr., 1953.
Brandon, Samuel G. F. *Creation Legends of the Ancient Near East.* London: Hodder & Stoughton, 1963.
Brown, Peter R. L. *The World of Late Antiquity: From Marcus Aurelius to Muhammad.* London: Thames & Hudson, 1971.

Černý, Jaroslav. *Ancient Egyptian Religion.* London: H.U.L., 1952.

Cochrane, Charles N. *Christianity and Classical Culture: A Study of Thought and Action from Augustus to Augustine.* London: Oxford Univ. Pr., 1944.

Cornford, Francis M. *Greek Religious Thought from Homer to the Age of Alexander.* London: Dent, 1923.

Dodds, Eric R. *The Greeks and the Irrational.* Berkeley: Univ. of California Pr., 1951.

—————. *Pagan and Christian in an Age of Anxiety: Some Aspects of Religious Experience from Marcus Aurelius to Constantine.* Cambridge: Cambridge Univ. Pr., 1965.

Duchesne-Guillemin, Jacques. *The Western Response to Zoroaster.* Oxford: Clarendon Pr., 1958.

Dumézil, Georges. *Archaic Roman Religion with an Appendix on the Religion of the Etruscans.* Tr. by Phillip Krapp. Chicago: Univ. of Chicago Pr., 1970. 2v.

Ferguson, John. *The Religions of the Roman Empire.* London: Thames & Hudson, 1970.

Festugière, André Marie Jean. *Personal Religion among the Greeks.* Berkeley: Univ. of California Pr., 1954.

Frankfort, Henri. *Ancient Egyptian Religion: An Interpretation.* New York: Columbia Univ. Pr., 1948.

—————. *Kingship and the Gods: A Study of Ancient Near Eastern Religion as the Integration of Society and Nature.* Chicago: Univ. of Chicago Pr., 1948.

—————, et al. *The Intellectual Adventure of Ancient Man: An Essay on Speculative Thought in the Ancient Near East.* Chicago: Univ. of Chicago Pr., 1948. Also published, in part, as *Before Philosophy.* Baltimore: Penguin, 1951.

Greene, William C. *Moira: Fate, Good, and Evil in Greek Thought.* Cambridge, Mass.: Harvard Univ. Pr., 1944.

Guthrie, William K. C. *The Greeks and Their Gods.* London: Methuen, 1962.

Hadas, Moses, and Morton Smith. *Heroes and Gods: Spiritual Biographies in Antiquity.* New York: Harper & Row, 1965.

Harris, Eve, and John R. Harris. *The Oriental Cults in Roman Britain.* Leiden: Brill, 1965.

Harrison, Jane E. *Prolegomena to the Study of Greek Religion.* 3d ed. Cambridge: Cambridge Univ. Pr., 1922.

Helmbold, Andrew K. *The Nag Hammadi Gnostic Texts and the Bible.* Grand Rapids, Mich.: Baker Book House, 1967.

Henning, Walter B. *Zoroaster: Politician or Witch Doctor?* London: Oxford Univ. Pr., 1951.

Hinnells, John R. *Persian Mythology.* London: Hamlyn, 1973.

—————, ed. *Mithraic Studies.* Manchester: Manchester Univ. Pr., 1973.

Hooke, Samuel H. *Babylonian and Assyrian Religion.* London: H.U.L., 1953.

—————, ed. *Myth, Ritual, and Kingship: Essays on the Theory and Practice of Kingship in the Ancient Near East and in Israel.* Oxford: Clarendon Pr., 1958.

Jaeger, Werner. *Paideia: The Ideals of Greek Culture.* New York: Oxford Univ. Pr., 1939–44. 3v.

James, Edwin O. *The Ancient Gods: The History and Diffusion of Religion in the Ancient Near East and the Eastern Mediterranean.* London: Weidenfeld & Nicolson, 1960.

Jonas, Hans. *The Gnostic Religion: The Message of the Alien God and the Beginnings of Christianity.* 2d ed. Boston: Beacon Pr., 1963.

Kerényi, Karl. *The Religion of the Greeks and Romans.* Tr. by Christopher Holme. London: Thames & Hudson, 1962.

Kirk, Geoffrey S. *Myth: Its Meaning and Functions in Ancient and Other Cultures.* Cambridge: Cambridge Univ. Pr., 1970.

Kramer, Samuel N. *Sumerian Mythology: A Study of Spiritual and Literary Achievement in the Third Millennium B.C.* Rev. ed. New York: Harper & Row, 1961.

————, ed. *Mythologies of the Ancient World.* Garden City, N.Y.: Doubleday, 1961.

Littleton, C. Scott. *The New Comparative Mythology: An Anthropological Assessment of the Theories of Georges Dumézil.* Berkeley: Univ. of California Pr., 1966.

MacMullen, Ramsay. *Enemies of the Roman Order: Treason, Unrest, and Alienation in the Empire.* Cambridge, Mass.: Harvard Univ. Pr., 1966.

Mercer, Samuel A. B. *The Religion of Ancient Egypt.* London: Luzac, 1949.

Morenz, Siegfried. *Egyptian Religion.* Tr. by Ann E. Keep. London: Methuen, 1973.

Murray, Gilbert. *Five Stages of Greek Religion.* 3d ed. Boston: Beacon Pr., 1951.

Nilsson, Martin P. *The Dionysiac Mysteries of the Hellenistic and Roman Age.* Lund: Gleerup, 1957.

————. *Greek Popular Religion.* New York: Columbia Univ. Pr., 1940. Reissued as *Greek Folk Religion.*

————. *A History of Greek Religion.* 2d ed. Tr. by F. J. Fielden. Oxford: Clarendon Pr., 1949.

Nock, Arthur Darby. *Conversion: The Old and the New in Religion from Alexander the Great to Augustine of Hippo.* London: Clarendon Pr., 1933.

Ogilvie, Robert M. *The Romans and Their Gods in the Age of Augustus.* London: Chatto and Windus, 1969.

Ringgren, Helmer. *Religions of the Ancient Near East.* London: S.P.C.K., 1973.

Rose, Herbert J. *Religion in Greece and Rome.* New York: Harper & Row, 1959.

Widengren, Geo. *Mani and Manichaeism.* Tr. by Charles Kessler. London: Weidenfeld & Nicolson, 1965.

Wright, G. Ernest, ed. *The Bible and the Ancient Near East: Essays in Honor of William Foxwell Albright.* Garden City, N.Y.: Doubleday, 1961.

Zaehner, Robert C. *The Dawn and Twilight of Zoroastrianism.* London: Weidenfeld & Nicolson, 1961.

ANCIENT ISRAEL, CLASSICAL JUDAISM, AND EARLY CHRISTIANITY

The religion of ancient Israel has long been a classical area of inquiry for Jewish and Christian scholars, as well as for historians and archaeologists. Modern literary critical studies of the Hebrew scriptures, or Christian Old Testament, began in the nineteenth century with the work of Julius Wellhausen. (See his *Prolegomena to the History of Ancient Israel* [1957] for the origin of this approach.) A standard one-volume summary of this literary approach is R. H. Pfeiffer, *Introduction to the Old Testament* (1941). Recent interest in the implications of archaeology for scholarly study of ancient Israel provided material for W. F. Albright, *From the Stone Age to Christianity: Monotheism and the Historical Process* (1957) and his *Archaeology and the Religion of Israel* (1959). Roland De Vaux, *Ancient Israel: Its Life and Institutions* (1961) and J. Pedersen, *Israel: Its Life and Culture* (1946–47) are comprehensive discussions of the social and cultural aspects of the subject.

Various scholarly points of view have been turned on ancient Israel's religion. W. O. E. Oesterley and T. H. Robinson, *Hebrew Religion: Its Origin and Development* (1930) represents a strictly evolutionary interpretation, while R. H. Pfeiffer, *Religion in the Old Testament: The History of a Spiritual Triumph* (1961) is a modified position, identifying two basic stages, one early and nationalistic, the other later and universalistic. Yehezkel Kaufmann, *The Religion of Israel: From Its Beginnings to the Babylonian Exile* (1960) represents a very different view. This study is the translation and abridgment of seven of a comprehensive eight volumes that painstakingly review Israel's development. Its thesis is that Israel's distinctive religious position was present from the outset of its history. *The History of Israel,* by Martin Noth (1958), and John Bright, *A History of Israel* (1959) are one-volume interpretations of ancient Israel's history that necessarily discuss its religious aspects in passing.

Judaism was a distinctive religion in the Hellenistic world. The subject is set in context by V. Tcherikover, *Hellenistic Civilization and the Jews* (1959). Literary sources may be supplemented through use of the materials assembled and analyzed in E. R. Goodenough, *Jewish Symbols in the Greco-Roman Period* (1953ff.). Studies of the significance of Hellenism for Judaism are presented in E. J. Bickerman's *From Ezra to the Last of the Maccabees: Foundations of Post-Biblical Judaism* (1962).

For a discussion of Josephus, a major Jewish writer who wrote in Greek, see Henry St. John Thackeray, *Josephus, the Man and the Historian* (1929) and selections with an introduction by N. N. Glatzer, *Rome and Jerusalem: The Writings of Josephus* (1960). Philo has been interpreted from different points of view. In his *By Light, Light: The Mystic Gospel of Hellenistic Judaism* (1935), E. R. Goodenough construed Judaism in the terms of the mystery religions. In contrast H. A. Wolfson, in *Philo: Foundations of Religious Philosophy in Judaism, Christianity, and Islam* (1947), holds that Philo translated central concerns of Judaism into the philosophical terms of Hellenistic culture.

Modern critical scholarship has made clear the extraordinary variety of Jewish practices between, broadly, the Babylonian captivity, which began with the sixth century before the common era (597), and the emergence of rabbinic Judaism as a classical version of the tradition after the destruction of the Temple by the Romans in the year 70. Jacob Neusner supplies a five-volume *History of the Jews in Babylonia* (1965–1970); also in a historical vein see N. N. Glatzer's abridgment of Emil Schürer, *A History of the Jewish People in the Time of Jesus* (1961). George F. Moore, *Judaism in the First Centuries of the Christian Era: The Age of the Tannaim* (1927, 1970) remains a basic discussion. The Pharisees have been interpreted sympathetically, as a counterweight to traditional Christian polemic in R. T. Herford, *The Pharisees* (1924) and Louis Finkelstein, *The Pharisees* (1962). The Messianic theme is important in Jewish literature of the period. J. Klausner, *The Messianic Idea in Israel* (1955) and W. D. Davies, *Torah in the Messianic Age and/or Age to Come* (1952) are especially relevant to Judaism, but also suggest one point of connection with the early Christians, who accepted Jesus as the Messiah.

Legendary materials that are available (see pages 148–54) suggest the substance of the piety of classical Judaism at the beginning of the common era. The work of Gershom Scholem makes evident the strong mystical strand in Judaism during this period. See his *Jewish Gnosticism, Merkabah Mysticism, and Talmudic Tradition* (1960). Hillel the Elder was central to the crystalization of rabbinic Judaism; see a biographical study by N. N. Glatzer, *Hillel the Elder: The Emergence of Classical Judaism* (1956). With the adoption of the Babylonian Talmud as the authoritative version, the rabbinic tradition was secure.

The discovery, after World War II, at Qumran on the Dead Sea of scrolls dating from the beginnings of the common era (or before) reawakened scholarly interest in those parties within the Jewish community of the Hellenistic world that failed to survive. The Dead Sea materials may be approached through Millar Burrows, *The Dead Sea Scrolls* (1955) and *More Light on the Dead Sea Scrolls: New Scrolls and New Interpretations* (1958). Frank M. Cross, Jr., has written a useful introduction, *The Ancient Library of Qumran and Modern Biblical Studies* (1958).

Early Christianity originated in this same matrix; indeed, from one perspective it was but a party or sect dissenting from pharisaic Judaism. Of course, the scholarly attention given not only to the scriptures of the early movement ("New" Testament), but also to the so-called intertestamental background, has been prodigious. R. H. Charles was the great master of these materials; see his survey titled *Religious Development between the Old and the New Testament* (1914). A more recent discussion is C. C. Torrey, *The Apocryphal Literature: A Brief Introduction* (1945). Discussions of the relationships between the Dead Sea community at Qumran and early Christians may be found in *The Scrolls and the New Testament*, edited by Krister Stendahl (1957) and also Jean Daniélou, *The Dead Sea Scrolls and Primitive Christianity* (1958).

The canon represents those writings judged by the early Church to embody the authentic traditions. Discussion of them, and by implication those excluded by early Christianity from the New Testament, may be found in B. F. Westcott, *A General Survey of the History of the Canon of the New Testament* (1881). The basic apocryphal literature—excluded from the canon—has been important to modern scholarship. The significance of more recent discoveries is discussed in Robert M. Grant and David N. Freedman, *The Secret Sayings of Jesus* (1960). The results of critical study of the canonical texts are summarized in Bruce M. Metzger, *The Text of the New Testament: Its Transmission, Corruption, and Restoration* (1968).

From the earliest years, the New Testament has been preeminently a church document, that is to say, subject to interpretation as the basis for the life of the institution. A survey of the development of interpretive points of view is available in Robert M. Grant, *The Bible in the Church: A Short History of Interpretation* (1948). One stage of that development has been the modern application of critical literary techniques to analysis of the New Testament. A useful comprehensive literary criticism of the early Christian writings is A. H. McNeile, *An Introduction to the Study of the New Testament* (1953).

In general, an especially close interrelationship has been posited between the first three gospels (or the "synoptics") while the fourth, John, is viewed as product of a relatively independent tradition. A classical study is found in B. H. Streeter, *The Four Gospels: A Study of Origins* (1924). A more recent introduction to this problem may be consulted in Frederick C. Grant, *The Gospels: Their Origin and Their Growth* (1957). A form critical approach to the Gospel materials, as an extension of the more strictly literary approach, developed between the World Wars. On this program, see R. Bultmann, *Form Criticism: A New Method of New Testament Research* (1934).

The Pauline literature has also been studied intensively. Useful discussions of this figure central to the development of early Christianity are A. D. Nock, *St. Paul* (1938) and John Knox, *Chapters in a Life of Paul* (1950).

The distinguished leaders of the early Christian community, in which the New Testament writings were identified as canonical during the second and third centuries, are known as the church fathers. In the early modern Church, large collections of patristic works were made, followed by ambitious translation projects in the nineteenth century, so that the writings of the fathers are generally accessible and critically studied. Discussion of the background of these materials is available in M. L. W. Laistner, *Christianity and Pagan Culture in the Later Roman Empire* (1951), and G. B. Caird, *The Apostolic Age* (1955).

For a brief history of the Church in this period, see Henry Chadwick, *The Early Church* (1967). More detailed studies are Philip Carrington, *The Early Christian Church* (1957) and W. H. C. Frend, *The Early Church* (1966). A stimulating discussion of the early Christian movement that makes use of modern social scientific theories and hypotheses is *Kingdom and Community: The Social World of Early Christianity* by John Gager (1975). Some specialized studies of particular aspects in the development of the Christian movement in this period are: J. N. D. Kelly, *Early Christian Doctrines* (1958); Jaroslav Pelikan, *The Emergence of the Catholic Tradition (to A.D. 600)* (1971—vol. 1 of a series); and H. A. Wolfson's *The Philosophy of the Church Fathers* (vol. 1, 1956). A majestic figure is discussed by Peter R. L. Brown in *Augustine of Hippo: A Biography* (1967).

Albright, W. F. *Archaeology and the Religion of Israel.* Baltimore, Md.: Johns Hopkins Pr., 1959.
———. *From the Stone Age to Christianity: Monotheism and the Historical Process.* Baltimore, Md.: Johns Hopkins Pr., 1957.

Bickerman, E. J. *From Ezra to the Last of the Maccabees: Foundations of Post-Biblical Judaism*. New York: Schocken Books, 1962.

Bright, John. *A History of Israel*. Philadelphia: Westminster Pr., 1959.

Brown, Peter R. L. *Augustine of Hippo: A Biography*. Berkeley: Univ. of California Pr., 1967.

Bultmann, R. *Form Criticism: A New Method of New Testament Research*. Tr. by F. C. Grant. Chicago: Willet, Clark, 1934.

Burrows, Millar. *The Dead Sea Scrolls*. New York: Viking, 1955.

————. *More Light on the Dead Sea Scrolls: New Scrolls and New Interpretations*. New York: Viking, 1958.

Caird, G. B. *The Apostolic Age*. London: Duckworth, 1955.

Carrington, Philip. *The Early Christian Church*. Cambridge: Cambridge Univ. Pr., 1957. 2v.

Chadwick, Henry. *The Early Church*. Baltimore, Md.: Penguin, 1967.

Charles, R. H. *Religious Development between the Old and the New Testament*. New York: Holt, Rinehart & Winston, 1914.

Cross, Frank M., Jr. *The Ancient Library of Qumran and Modern Biblical Studies*. Garden City, N.Y.: Doubleday, 1958.

Daniélou, Jean. *The Dead Sea Scrolls and Primitive Christianity*. Tr. by S. Attanasio. Baltimore, Md.: Helicon Pr., 1958.

Davies, W. D. *Torah in the Messianic Age and/or Age to Come*. Philadelphia: Soc. of Biblical Literature, 1952.

De Vaux, Roland. *Ancient Israel: Its Life and Institutions*. Tr. by J. McHugh. New York: McGraw-Hill, 1961.

Finkelstein, Louis. *The Pharisees*. Philadelphia: Jewish Publication Soc., 1962. 2v.

Frend, W. H. C. *The Early Church*. Philadelphia: Lippincott, 1966.

Gager, John. *Kingdom and Community: The Social World of Early Christianity*. Englewood Cliffs, N.J.: Prentice-Hall, 1975.

Ginsberg, Louis. *Legends of the Bible*. Philadelphia: Jewish Publication Soc.; New York: Simon & Schuster, 1956.

Glatzer, N. N. *Hillel the Elder: The Emergence of Classical Judaism*. New York: B'nai B'rith Hillel Foundations, 1956.

————. "Introduction," *Rome and Jerusalem: The Writings of Josephus*. Ed. by Glatzer. New York: Meridian Books, 1960.

Goldin, Judah. *The Living Talmud: The Wisdom of the Fathers*. Chicago: Univ. of Chicago Pr., 1958.

Goodenough, E. R. *By Light, Light: The Mystic Gospel of Hellenistic Judaism*. New Haven, Conn.: Yale Univ. Pr., 1935.

————. *Jewish Symbols in the Greco-Roman Period*. Vol. 1– . New York: Princeton, 1953– . (Bollingen series.)

Grant, Frederick C. *The Gospels: Their Origin and Their Growth*. New York: Harper & Row, 1957.

Grant, Robert M. *The Bible in the Church: A Short History of Interpretation*. New York: Macmillan, 1948.

————, and David H. Freedman. *The Secret Sayings of Jesus*. Garden City, N.Y.: Doubleday, 1960.

Herford, R. T. *The Pharisees*. London: Allen & Unwin, 1924.

Kaufmann, Yehezkel. *The Religion of Israel: From Its Beginnings to the Babylonian Exile.* Chicago: Univ. of Chicago Pr., 1960.

Kelly, J. N. D. *Early Christian Doctrines.* London: A. and C. Black, 1958.

Klausner, J. *The Messianic Idea in Israel.* New York: Macmillan, 1955.

Knox, John. *Chapters in a Life of Paul.* New York: Abingdon Pr., 1950.

Laistner, M. L. W. *Christianity and Pagan Culture in the Later Roman Empire.* Ithaca, N.Y.: Cornell Univ. Pr., 1951.

McNeile, A. H. *An Introduction to the Study of the New Testament.* 2d rev. ed. Ed. by C. S. C. Williams. Oxford: Clarendon Pr., 1953.

Metzger, Bruce M. *The Text of the New Testament: Its Transmission, Corruption, and Restoration.* 2d ed. Oxford: Oxford Univ. Pr., 1968.

Montefiore, C. G., and H. Loewe. *A Rabbinic Anthology.* Philadelphia: Jewish Publication Soc., 1960.

Moore, George F. *Judaism in the First Centuries of the Christian Era: The Age of the Tannaim.* Cambridge, Mass.: Harvard Univ. Pr., 1927, 1970. 3v.

Neusner, Jacob. *A History of the Jews in Babylonia.* Leiden: Brill, 1965–70. 5v.

Nock, A. D. *St. Paul.* London: Butterworth, 1938.

Noth, Martin. *The History of Israel.* Tr. by S. Goodman. London: A. and C. Black, 1958.

Oesterley, W. O. E., and T. H. Robinson. *Hebrew Religion: Its Origin and Development.* New York: Macmillan, 1930.

Pedersen, J. *Israel: Its Life and Culture.* Oxford: Oxford Univ. Pr., 1946–47. 4v. in 2.

Pelikan, Jaroslav. *The Emergence of the Catholic Tradition (to A.D. 600).* Chicago: Univ. of Chicago Pr., 1971. (The Christian Tradition, vol. 1)

Pfeiffer, R. H. *Introduction to the Old Testament.* New York: Harper & Row, 1941.

———. *Religion in the Old Testament: The History of a Spiritual Triumph.* Ed. by C. C. Forman. New York: Harper, 1961.

Scholem, Gershom. *Jewish Gnosticism, Merkabah Mysticism, and Talmudic Tradition.* New York: Jewish Theological Seminary, 1960.

Schürer, Emil. *A History of the Jewish People in the Time of Jesus.* Abridged by N. N. Glatzer. New York: Schocken Books, 1961.

Stendahl, Krister, ed. *The Scrolls and the New Testament.* New York: Harper, 1957.

Streeter, B. H. *The Four Gospels: A Study of Origins.* London: Macmillan, 1924.

Tcherikover, V. *Hellenistic Civilization and the Jews.* Tr. by S. Applebaum. Philadelphia: Jewish Publication Soc., 1959.

Thackeray, Henry St. John. *Josephus, the Man and the Historian.* New York: Jewish Institute of Religion Pr., 1929.

Torrey, C. C. *The Apocryphal Literature: A Brief Introduction.* New Haven, Conn.: Yale Univ. Pr., 1945.

Wellhausen, Julius. *Prolegomena to the History of Ancient Israel.* (E. T.) Toronto: Longmans, Green, 1957.

Westcott, B. F. *A General Survey of the History of the Canon of the New Testament.* London: Macmillan, 1881.

Wolfson, H. A. *Philo: Foundations of Religious Philosophy in Judaism, Christianity, and Islam.* Cambridge, Mass.: Harvard Univ. Pr., 1947. 2v.
————. *The Philosophy of the Church Fathers.* Vol. 1. Cambridge, Mass.: Harvard Univ. Pr., 1956.

ISLAM AS A RELIGIOUS TRADITION

Islam developed in the seventh century of the common era among the Bedouins of the Arabian Peninsula. The movement spread rapidly and became a dominant force in the Middle East and through much of the Mediterranean basin. Meanwhile Judaism continued its diaspora existence and the centers of Christian influence moved to the Eastern Empire as well as Western Europe.

There are a number of useful general introductions to Islam written from different perspectives. A slight volume by Sir H. A. R. Gibb, *Mohammedanism: An Historical Survey* (1961) has been widely used since its publication. A comprehensive three-volume discussion of the civilization by Marshall G. S. Hodgson is currently published under the title *The Venture of Islam: Conscience and History in a World Civilization* (1974). A discussion of Islam that incorporates a significant number of illustrative texts is John A. Williams, *Islam* (1961). See also his *Themes of Islamic Civilization* (1971). Another introduction to the founder and his movement that includes texts is Arthur Jeffery (editor), *Islam: Muhammed and His Religion* (1958); see also his *A Reader on Islam* (1962). Finally, *Islam: The Straight Path* (1958), edited by Kenneth Morgan, presents essays written about Islam by followers of the movement.

Surveys of the Arabs comment on the characteristics of their pre-Islamic history as well as the impact made by the rise of Islam upon their society. For a general discussion of the background, see especially Philip K. Hitti's *History of the Arabs* (1970) and Bernard Lewis, *The Arabs in History* (1966). More specialized consideration of various issues include the following: An older study of pre-Islamic Arabia is found in DeLacy O'Leary's *Arabia before Muhammad* (1927); W. Robertson Smith's *Lectures on the Religion of the Semites* (1889 and 1956), an early and extremely influential study, remains a useful review of the specifically religious aspects of Semitic society (readers need to be skeptical about his argument that sacrifice is a form of communion with deity); Marshall G. S. Hodgson discussed the relationship of Islam to earlier Arabian religion in *The*

Venture of Islam (vol. 1); see also Ibn al-Kalbī, *The Book of Idols* (1952) for an early Islamic reflection on preceding religion. Discussion of "Islam" as a term for the faith of followers of Muhammad, the Prophet, is available in Helmer Ringgren's *Islam, 'aslama, and Muslim* (1949).

Muhammad, who lived circa 570 to 632 of the common era, received his commission and served as a prophet to his people for the last two decades of his life. The *Qur'ān* is the series of revelations made to him, on the basis of which his mission developed. In the several decades he served as the Chosen Prophet, Arabia was united under his leadership. Muhammad and his role have been magnified through story and legend within the Muslim community. The impulse to create biographies of the Prophet has been strong, especially in the last century, but these writings do not rest upon critical scholarship.

Critical biographical study of Muhammad began among European scholars in the nineteenth century. This move to reflect on and assess sources is presented in Sir William Muir, *The Life of Mohammad* (1861, 1912). Studies by W. Montgomery Watt have drawn back from extreme skepticism about the worth of the traditional sources, a critical stance that was inevitable once modern perspectives were introduced: see *Muhammad: Prophet and Statesman* (1961). Watt has also emphasized the relationships between the Prophet, his movement, and social conditions. A study with related interests is Maxime Rodinson, *Mohammad* (1971).

Critical scholarship has also emphasized the question of religious influences on the movement. This impulse may be seen in C. C. Torrey, *The Jewish Foundation of Islam* (1933). A subsequent study by Abraham I. Katsh also explored Jewish sources: see *Judaism in Islam* (1954). Tör Andrae, *Mohammad the Man and His Faith* (1934) argued that parallels to monophysite Christianity are significant. On Christian influence see an older work, Richard Bell, *The Origin of Islam in Its Christian Environment* (1926). A useful summary of article literature on the Prophet is James E. Royster, "The Study of Muhammad: A Survey of Approaches from the Perspective of the History and Phenomenology of Religion."

In certain logical respects, the Qur'ān is more central to Islam than the life of the Prophet, for Muhammad was but the vehicle for definitive expression of the divine will. So high are the claims made about the Qur'ān that Muslims considered it to be the very words of God, possibly even eternally existing beside the deity. Such extreme claims render translation problematical for true members of Islam, although numerous versions have been made available. A. J. Arberry, *The Koran Interpreted* (1955) and selections entitled *The Holy Koran* (1953) include reflections on the problems of translation.

Religiously considered, Islamic writing (in an inclusive sense) is viewed as elaboration of the fundamental divine revelation. But within the Islamic writings a technical literature is specifically dedicated to interpreting the Qur'ān, although little of it has been made accessible in translation. For an example of this genre, see a modern commentary in English by Muhammad 'Ali, *The Holy Qur'ān* (1951). This pattern continues as Islamic practice; see the discussion by J. J. G. Jansen, *The Interpretation of the Koran in Modern Egypt* (1974).

Western critical scholars have been concerned with the Qur'ān since the late nineteenth century. Their work has proceeded both along the lines of text criticism and in terms of pursuing questions central to higher criticism. See Richard Bell, *The Qur'ān* (1937–39) and a companion volume, issued in a revised and enlarged edition by W. Montgomery Watt, *Bell's Introduction to the Qur'ān* (1970). A broader discussion of Muslim scripture is found in Kenneth Cragg, *The Event of the Qur'ān: Islam in Its Scripture* (1971). A related consideration of its contents by the same author is *The Mind of the Qur'ān: Chapters in Reflection* (1973). In the last two decades, linguistic analysis has been appropriated to study of the Qur'ānic text. Especially see the work of Toshihiko Izutsu, *The Structure of the Ethical Terms in the Koran* (1959; see also a revised version, *Ethico-Religious Concepts in the Qur'ān* 1966). A comparable study is *God of Justice: A Study on the Ethical Doctrine of the Qur'ān* by Daud Rahbar (1960). In *The Qur'ān as Scripture* (1952), Arthur Jeffery discussed the special characteristics of the Muslim scripture.

The aspect of the tradition concerned with Muhammad's exemplary actions is known as *hadīth,* for in religious terms it is unthinkable that there should be a dichotomy between the prophet's role as vehicle for revelation and his actions. Critical study of this literature rests on the monumental scholarship by Ignaz Goldziher, first published in the nineteenth century. See volume 2 of his *Muslim Studies* (edited by S. M. Stern, 1971). His work may also be approached through Alfred Guillaume's *The Traditions of Islam* (1924). More recently, the central issues of the basis for hadīth literature have been approached in different ways. See Fazlur Rahman, *Islamic Methodology in History* (1965), Nabia Abbott, *Studies in Arabic Literary*

Papryi (1957), and G. H. A. Juynboll, *The Authenticity of the Tradition Literature* (1969).

The Islamic tradition does not include a highly developed aspect broadly comparable to theology in Western Christianity. For a basic essay on this question, see H. A. R. Gibb, "The Structure of Religious Thought in Islam," available in S. J. Shaw and W. R. Polk, *Studies on the Civilization of Islam* (1962). An introduction to the subject in the first several hundred years of the movement is by Francis E. Peters; his *Allah's Commonwealth: A History of Islam in the Near East, 600–1100* (1973) relates religious thought to political developments. See the following studies, which give attention to several aspects of this question: A. J. Wensinck, *The Muslim Creed* (1932); A. S. Tritton, *Muslim Theology* (1947); W. Montgomery Watt, *Free Will and Predestination in Early Islam* (1948); and his *The Formative Record of Islamic Thought* (1973).

Although it is not useful to compare Muslim theology to systematic Christian religious thought, there is a tradition of philosophical writing that at least superficially resembles philosophical study of religion in a Western sense. The *fasyah* were a small intellectual group, finally repudiated by the broader community; thus the periodic leavening of religious thought, so typical within Christian settings, was not present within Islam. Two monographs with broader implications are A. J. Arberry, *Relevation and Reason in Islam* (1957) and Fazlur Rahman, *Prophecy in Islam* (1958). Other studies, narrowly focused in specific areas, include DeLacy O'Leary, *Arabic Thought and Its Place in History* (1922) and W. Montgomery Watt, *Muslim Intellectual: A Study of Al-Ghazālī* (1963). Muhsin Mahdī, *Ibn Khaldūn's Philosophy of History* (1957) is another specific study that relates to the broader question.

Muslim law is especially important, since behavior or practice is, if anything, a more fundamental religious impulse than belief or reflection. Comprehensive discussions are Joseph Schacht, *An Introduction to Islamic Law* (1964) and Noel J. Coulson, *A History of Islamic Law* (1964). On the question of the development of this tradition see *The Origins of Muhammedan Jurisprudence* (1950), also by Joseph Schacht.

The four schools of teachings are compared by Abdul Rabinov in *Principles of Muhammadan Jurisprudence* (1911). The adaptation that has taken place in the period of contact with the modern West is surveyed by James N. D. Anderson in *Islamic Law in the Modern World* (1959). The cognate question, how Muslims relate to the religious and governmental authorities, is probed by S. D. Goitein in "Attitudes toward Government in Islam and Judaism" in *Studies in Islamic History and Institutions* (1966). An ambitious summary discussion is Erwin I. J. Rosenthal, *Political Thought in Medieval Islam* (1958).

Reuben Levy, *The Social Structure of Islam* (1957) and Henri Lammens, *Islam: Beliefs and Institutions* (1929) summarize the religious practices of those who follow Islam. Beyond the obligation to the "pillars" (confession of faith, prayer, alms giving, fasting in Ramadhān and pilgrimage to Mecca) there are a number of aspects of piety that deserve notice. The following studies are examples as indicated by title: G. E. von Grunebaum, *Muhammadan Festivals* (1951); Duncan B. MacDonald, *The Religious Attitude and Life in Islam* (1909); and Constance Padwick, *Muslim Devotions* (1961). H. Granquist summarizes practices connected with death in his *Muslim Death and Burial* (1965).

Two schools, the Sunnīs and the Shī'ah, have been part of Islamic life since its beginnings. The former understand themselves as followers of the tradition in a direct and inclusive way, while the Shī'ah originated as partisans of Ali, son-in-law of the Prophet. The distinction between orthodox and heterodox, while often utilized to discuss these parties, presents difficulties when applied to these schools. On the Shī'ah, see *The Shī'ite Religion* by Dwight M. Donaldson (1933).

Sufism represented the development of a pronounced mystical vein in Islam. By early in the second Christian millennium, Sufism had become pervasive and strong—and it retains its hold into the modern era. See Reynold A. Nicholson, *The Mystics of Islam* (1914), and A. J. Arberry, *Sufism* (1950). Annemarie Schimmel, *Mystical Dimensions of Islam* (1975) has recently become available. Among related studies, see Reynold A. Nicholson, *Studies in Islamic Mysticism* (1921) and his *The Idea of Personality in Sūfism* (1923). For a selection of Sufi materials, see Margaret Smith, *Readings from the Mystics of Islam* (1950) and *Studies in Early Mysticism in the Near and Middle East* (1931), in which the question of origins is reviewed. The brotherhoods are studied in J. S. Trimingham, *The Sufi Orders in Islam* (1971).

The internal development of Islam in the modern period has been distinctive, especially as a result of intensive interaction with European cultures. H. A. R. Gibb, *Modern Trends in Islam* (1947) and Wilfred C. Smith, *Islam in Modern History* (1957) are useful. Of course, divisions within the Muslim world mean that there has been a differential impact on Islamic thought and practice. The following studies suggest the range of developments of Islam in different regions. On Turkey, see Bernard Lewis, *The Emergence of Modern Turkey* (1961) and Niyazi Berkes, *The Development of Secularism in Turkey* (1964). Charles C. Adams, *Islam and Modernism in Egypt* (1933) and Albert H. Hourani, *Arabic Thought in the Liberal Age, 1798–1939* (1962) are directed to Egypt in particular. *Modern Islam in India,* by Wilfred C. Smith (1946), together with Ishtiaq Husayn Qureshi, *The Muslim Community of the Indo-Pakistan Subcontinent (610–1947)* (1962), Muhammad Mujib, *The Indian Muslims* (1967), and Aziz Ahmad, *Islamic Modernism in India and Pakistan, 1857–1964* (1967) discuss that subcontinent.

The development of Islam in Indonesia may be reviewed in the following studies (among others): Deliar Noer, *The Modernist Muslim Movement in Indonesia, 1900–1942* (1973) and Harry J. Benda, *Continuity and Change in Indonesian Islam* (1965). Especially to be noted are two studies by a distinguished anthropologist, Clifford Geertz: *The Religion of Java* (1960), an ethnographic study, and his comparison of Islam in Indonesia and Morocco, *Islam Observed* (1968).

Abbott, Nabia. *Studies in Arabic Literary Papyri.* Chicago: Univ. of Chicago Pr., 1957. 3v.

Adams, Charles C. *Islam and Modernism in Egypt.* London: Oxford Univ. Pr., 1933.

'Ali, Muhammad. *The Holy Qur'ān.* 4th rev. ed. Lahore, 1951.

Anderson, James N. D. *Islamic Law in the Modern World.* New York: New York Univ. Pr., 1959.

Andrae, Tör. *Mohammed, the Man and His Faith.* Tr. by Theophil Menzel. New York: Barnes & Noble, 1934.

Arberry, A. J. *The Holy Koran: An Introduction with Selections.* London: Allen & Unwin, 1953.

———. *The Koran Interpreted.* London: Allen & Unwin, 1955. 2v.

———. *Revelation and Reason in Islam.* London: Allen & Unwin, 1957.

———. *Sufism, An Account of the Mystics of Islam.* London: Allen & Unwin, 1950.

Aziz Ahmad. *Islamic Modernism in India and Pakistan, 1857–1964.* London: Oxford Univ. Pr., 1967.

Bell, Richard. *The Origin of Islam in Its Christian Environment.* London: Macmillan, 1926.

———. *The Qur'ān.* Edinburgh: T. and T. Clark, 1937–39. 2v.

Benda, Harry J. *Continuity and Change in Indonesian Islam.* New Haven, Conn.: Yale Univ. Pr., 1965.

Berkes, Niyazi. *The Development of Secularism in Turkey.* Montreal: McGill Univ. Pr., 1964.

Coulson, Noel J. *A History of Islamic Law*. Edinburgh: Edinburgh Univ. Pr., 1964.

Cragg, Kenneth. *The Event of the Qur'ān: Islam in Its Scripture*. London: Allen & Unwin, 1971.

———. *The Mind of the Qur'ān: Chapters in Reflection*. London: Allen & Unwin, 1973.

Donaldson, Dwight M. *The Shi'ite Religion; A History of Islam in Persia and Irak*. London: Luzac, 1933.

Geertz, Clifford. *Islam Observed; Religious Development in Morocco and Indonesia*. New Haven, Conn.: Yale Univ. Pr., 1968.

———. *The Religion of Java*. Glencoe, Ill.: Free Pr., 1960.

Gibb, Sir H. A. R. *Modern Trends in Islam*. Chicago: Univ. of Chicago Pr., 1947.

———. *Mohammedanism: An Historical Survey*. London: Oxford Univ. Pr., 1961.

———. "The Structure of Religious Thought in Islam." In *Studies on the Civilization of Islam*, ed. by Shaw and Polk. Boston: Beacon Pr., 1962.

Goitein, S. D. "Attitudes toward Government in Islam and Judaism." In *Studies in Islamic History and Institutions*. Leiden: Brill, 1966.

Goldziher, Ignaz. *Muslim Studies*. Ed. by S. M. Stern. London: Allen, 1968–71. 2v.

Granquist, H. *Muslim Death and Burial*. Helsinki: Societas Scientiarium Fennica, 1965.

Grunebaum, G. E. von. *Muhammedan Festivals*. New York: Schuman, 1951.

Guillaume, Alfred. *The Traditions of Islam*. Oxford: Clarendon Pr., 1924.

Hitti, Philip K. *History of the Arabs*. 10th ed. London: Macmillan, 1970.

Hodgson, Marshall G. S. *The Venture of Islam: Conscience and History in a World Civilization*. Vol. 1. Chicago: Univ. of Chicago Pr., 1974.

Hourani, Albert H. *Arabic Thought in the Liberal Age, 1798–1939*. London: Oxford Univ. Pr., 1962.

Ibn al-Kalbī. *The Book of Idols*. Tr. by Habīh Amīn Fāris. Princeton, N.J.: Princeton Univ. Pr., 1952.

Izutsu, Toshihiko. *The Structure of the Ethical Terms in the Koran*. Tokyo: Keiō Institute, 1959. Rev. ed.: *Ethico-Religious Concepts in the Qur'ān*. Montreal: McGill Univ. Pr., 1966.

Jansen, J. J. G. *The Interpretation of the Koran in Modern Egypt*. Leiden: Brill, 1974.

Jeffery, Arthur. *The Qur'ān as Scripture*. New York: Moore, 1952.

———, ed. *Islam: Muhammed and His Religion*. New York: Liberal Arts Pr., 1958.

———, ed. *A Reader on Islam*. 's-Gravenhage, Netherlands: Mouton, 1962.

Juynboll, G. H. A. *The Authenticity of the Tradition Literature*. Leiden: Brill, 1969.

Katsh, Abraham I. *Judaism in Islam*. New York: Block, 1954.

Lammens, Henri. *Islam: Beliefs and Institutions*. Tr. by E. Denison Ross. London: Methuen, 1929.

Levy, Reuben. *The Social Structure of Islam*. Cambridge: Cambridge Univ. Pr., 1957.

Lewis, Bernard. *The Arabs in History*. London: Hutchinson, 1966.
———. *The Emergence of Modern Turkey*. London: Oxford Univ. Pr., 1961.
MacDonald, Duncan B. *The Religious Attitude and Life in Islam*. Chicago: Univ. of Chicago Pr., 1909.
Mahdī, Mushin. *Ibn Khaldūn's Philosophy of History*. London: Allen & Unwin, 1957.
McNeill, William H., and Marilyn Waldman, eds. *The Islamic World*. New York: Oxford Univ. Pr., 1973.
Morgan, Kenneth, ed. *Islam: The Straight Path*. New York: Ronald, 1958.
Muír, William. *The Life of Mohammed*. (1861). Rev. ed. Edinburgh: Grant, 1912.
Mujib, Muhammad. *The Indian Muslims*. Montreal: McGill, 1967.
Nicholson, Reynold A. *The Idea of Personality in Sūfism*. Cambridge: Cambridge Univ. Pr., 1923.
———. *The Mystics of Islam*. London: Bell & Sons, 1914.
———. *Studies in Islamic Mysticism*. Cambridge: Cambridge Univ. Pr., 1921.
Noer, Deliar. *The Modernist Muslim Movement in Indonesia 1900–1942*. Singapore: Oxford Univ. Pr., 1973.
O'Leary, DeLacy. *Arabia before Muhammad*. London: Kegan Paul, 1927.
———. *Arabic Thought and Its Place in History*. London: Routledge & Kegan Paul, 1922.
Padwick, Constance. *Muslim Devotions*. London: S.P.C.K., 1961.
Peters, Francis E. *Allah's Commonwealth: A History of Islam in the Near East, 600–1100*. New York: Simon & Schuster, 1973.
Qureshi, Ishtiaq Husayn. *The Muslim Community of the Indo-Pakistan Subcontinent (610–1947)*. 's-Gravenhage, Netherlands: Mouton, 1962.
Rabinov, Abdul. *Principles of Muhammadan Jurisprudence*. London: Luzac, 1911.
Rahbar, Daud. *God of Justice: A Study on the Ethical Doctrine of the Qur'ān*. Leiden: Brill, 1960.
Rahman, Fazlur. *Islamic Methodology in History*. Karachi: Central Institute of Islamic Research, 1965.
———. *Prophecy in Islam*. London: Allen & Unwin, 1958.
Ringgren, Helmer. *Islam, 'aslama, and Muslim*. Uppsala: Gleerup, 1949.
Rodinson, Maxime. *Mohammed*. Tr. by Anne Carter. New York: Pantheon Books, 1971.
Rosenthal, Erwin I. J. *Political Thought in Medieval Islam*. Cambridge: Cambridge Univ. Pr., 1958.
Royster, James E. "The Study of Muhammad: A Survey of Approaches from the Perspective of the History and Phenomenology of Religion." *Muslim World* 62:49–70 (1972).
Schacht, Joseph. *An Introduction to Islamic Law*. Oxford: Clarendon Pr., 1964.
———. *The Origins of Muhammedan Jurisprudence*. Oxford: Clarendon Pr., 1950.
Schimmel, Annemarie. *Mystical Dimensions of Islam*. Chapel Hill: Univ. of North Carolina Pr., 1975.

Shaw, S. J., and W. R. Polk. *Studies on the Civilization of Islam*. Boston: Beacon Pr., 1962.

Smith, Margaret. *Readings from the Mystics of Islam*. London: Luzac, 1950.

———. *Studies in Early Mysticism in the Near and Middle East*. New York: Macmillan, 1931.

Smith, W. Robertson. *Lectures on the Religion of the Semites*. Edinburgh, 1889. Repr.: New York: Meridian Books, 1956.

Smith, Wilfred C. *Islam in Modern History*. Princeton, N.J.: Princeton Univ. Pr., 1957.

———. *Modern Islam in India*. London: Gollancz, 1946.

Torrey, C. C. *The Jewish Foundation of Islam*. New York: Jewish Institute of Religion, 1933.

Trimingham, J. S. *The Sufi Orders in Islam*. Oxford: Clarendon Pr., 1971.

Tritton, A. S. *Muslim Theology*. London: Luzac, 1947.

Watt, W. Montgomery. *The Formative Record of Islamic Thought*. Edinburgh: Edinburgh Univ. Pr., 1973.

———. *Free Will and Predestination in Early Islam*. London: Luzac, 1948.

———. *Muhammad, Prophet and Statesman*. London: Oxford Univ. Pr., 1961.

———. *Muslim Intellectual: A Study of Al-Ghazālī*. Edinburgh: Edinburgh Univ. Pr., 1963.

———, ed. and rev. *Bell's Introduction to the Qur'ān*. Edinburgh: Edinburgh Univ. Pr., 1970.

Wensinck, A. J. *The Muslim Creed: Its Genesis and Historical Development*. Cambridge: Cambridge Univ. Pr., 1932.

Williams, John A., ed. *Islam*. New York: Braziller, 1961.

———. *Themes of Islamic Civilization*. Berkeley: Univ. of California Pr., 1971.

3

Religious Traditions
in the West

By the seventh century of the common era, the Talmudic tradition of Babylonia became generally authoritative for the Jewish community, thus reducing the internal variety and pluralism of the practices noted in the classical period. When, in turn, the central role of this tradition ceased in the eleventh century, European Jewish life came to predominate within the broader tradition, although there were also centers of influence in numerous locations outside Europe. Surveys or overviews of this time include Isidore Epstein, *Judaism: A Historical Presentation* (1959), Arthur Hertzberg, *Judaism* (1961), N. N. Glatzer, *A Jewish Reader: In Time and Eternity* (1961), and Jacob Neusner, *The Way of Torah: An Introduction to Judaism* (1970). For a series of essays on approaches to the subject, see *The Study of Judaism: Bibliographical Essays,* by the Anti-Defamation League of B'nai B'rith (1972). A magisterial multivolume study by Salo Baron, *A Social and Religious History of the Jews* (1952–) is comprehensive, and individual volumes are useful for this period. See also an earlier and shorter version of Baron's survey (1937) and relevant sections of his *The Jewish Community* (1942). Finally, *Great Ages and Ideas of the Jewish People,* edited by L. W. Schwartz (1956), may be useful.

The richness and variety of the tradition is indicated in historical accounts of particular periods or facets of Jewish life. Among many other books the following may be useful: S. D. Goitein, *Jews and Arabs* (1964); Israel Abrahams, *Jewish Life in the Middle Ages* (1958); Yitzhak Baer, *A History of the Jews in Christian Spain*

63

(1961); Cecil Roth, *A History of the Marranos* (1941), *The History of the Jews of Italy* (1946), *The Jews in the Renaissance* (1959), and *A History of the Jews in England* (1949). Guido Kisch writes of *The Jews in Medieval Germany* (1970).

On the special subject of anti-Semitism in Europe, see Edward H. Flannery, *The Anguish of the Jews* (1965), and a series of studies by James Parkes: *The Conflict of the Church and the Synagogue* (1961), *The Jew in the Medieval Community* (1938), and *Judaism and Christianity* (1948). Leon Poliakov is publishing a comprehensive account, *The History of Anti-Semitism* (in progress; 1965, 1973).

The Talmud, itself a commentary on the Mishnah (which is understood as a commentary on the Torah), has also been the subject of extensive commentary. See appropriate sections in Louis Ginsberg, *On Jewish Law and Lore* (1955) and Bernard M. Casper, *An Introduction to Jewish Bible Commentary* (1960). Two towering medieval figures were Maimonedes and Joseph Karo.

Explicitly religious practices and materials may be approached through Abraham Millgram, *Jewish Worship* (1971) and *An Anthology of Medieval Hebrew Literature* (1961); also N. N. Glatzer, *Language of Faith* (1967). Theodore H. Gaster has discussed customs in *Customs and Folkways of Jewish Life* (1955) and also *Festivals of the Jewish Year* (1953). For related studies, see Joshua Trachtenberg, *Jewish Magic and Superstition* (1939), and Louis M. Epstein, *Sex Laws and Customs in Judaism* (1948).

Jewish mysticism has been studied extensively by Gershom Scholem. For an introduction, see *Major Trends in Jewish Mysticism* (1941); also *Kabbalah* (1974). Another introduction is Ernst Mueller, *A History of Jewish Mysticism* (1946). The development of Messianic concerns is reviewed in Julius H. Greenstone, *The Messiah Idea in Jewish History* (1906) and Joseph Sarachek, *The Doctrine of the Messiah in Medieval Jewish Literature* (1968). Attention is given to methods of calculating the "times" in Abba Hillel Silver, *History of Messianic Speculation in Israel* (1927). Also see Gershom Scholem, *The Messianic Idea in Judaism* (1971) and *Sabbatai Sevi* (1973). In the former, Scholem discusses connections of Messianism with Hasidism. See also Martin Buber, *The Origin and Meaning of Hasidism* (1966) and *The Tales of the Hasidim* (1947–48). Jerome R. Mintz, *Legends of the Hasidim* (1968) and Louis I. Newman (editor), *The Hasidic Anthology* (1963), also make materials available.

The place of the Jews in modern European societies and the development of several versions of Judaism as religions are complex and perennially interesting subjects. Raphael Mahler, *Jewish Emancipation* (1941) presents materials from the seventeenth century to World War I, while N. N. Glatzer has edited *The Dynamics of Emancipation* (1965), which covers the nineteenth and twentieth centuries. On eighteenth- and early nineteenth-century Germany, see Michael A. Meyer, *The Origins of the Modern Jew* (1967). *The French Enlightenment and the Jews* (1968) byArthur Hertzberg is a major work. Alexander Altmann, *Studies in Nineteenth-Century Jewish Intellectual History* (1964) contains relevant essays; Salo Baron has written on *The Russian Jew under Tsars and Soviets* (1964).

The major Jewish figure to embrace the Enlightenment, and coincidentally the understanding of religion in a modern sense, was Moses Mendelssohn; see his biography by Alexander Altmann (1973). Mendelssohn's writings were translated and edited by Alfred Jospe in *Jerusalem and Other Jewish Writings* (1969). Reform Judaism was the most radical attempt to return to an essential prophetic biblical version of the tradition under the impact of modern culture. An early study, *The Reform Movement in Judaism,* by David Philipson, was published in a revised edition in 1931. Joseph L. Blau has published representative materials in *Reform Judaism* (1973).

A less radical version of the Reform impulse has become established in the United States as Conservative Judaism. Moshe Davis, *The Emergence of Conservative Judaism: The Historical School in 19th Century America* (1963), and Marshall Sklare's *Conservative Judaism* (1972) are relatively recent studies. The Reconstructionist proposal is a wholly American movement, which may be approached through the writings of its founder, Mordecai Kaplan. See his *Judaism as a Civilization* (1967).

Orthodox Judaism, while adopting the stance of preserving and continuing the ancient traditions, no less represents a religious development of it. For the East European world of Judaism, see the edited volume by Lucy Davidowicz, *The Golden Tradition* (1967). Maurice Samuel, *The World of Scholom Aleichem* (1943), also portrays this world. For the American expression of this impulse, see *Studies in Judaica,* edited by Leon D. Stitskin (1974). Solomon Poll, *The Hasidic Community of Williamsburg* (1962) is a study of the Eastern European Jewish community transplanted to Brooklyn. Zionism represents at least a quasi-religious strand in modern Jewish life. It is accessible in Arthur Hertzberg (editor), *The Zionist Idea* (1972).

Summary discussions of American Judaism are available in Joseph

L. Blau, *Judaism in America: From Curiosity to Third Faith* (1976), Nathan Glazer, *American Judaism* (1972), and Marshall Sklare, *America's Jews* (1971). (For the religious context of Judaism in American society, see the section later in the essay on the study of religion in American history.)

In certain respects, religious thought within Judaism in the last century has been parallel to, and developed points of connection with, Christian counterparts. References are given in the discussion of religious thought, but in this section attention should be called to the following figures. N. N. Glatzer has written a biography of *Franz Rosenzweig: His Life and Thought* (1953). For the latter's major work, see *The Star of Redemption* (1971). Martin Buber may be approached through Malcolm L. Diamond, *Martin Buber* (1960) and Maurice Friedman, *Martin Buber* (1955). Buber's numerous writings, readily available in the United States, include *I and Thou* (1958) and three collections of essays: *On Judaism,* edited by N. N. Glatzer (1967), *Israel and the World* (1948), and *Eclipse of God* (1952). See also the selection of materials by N. N. Glatzer, *On the Bible* (1968). Contemporary perspectives are available in the reader *Faith and Reason: Essays in Judaism,* edited by Robert Gordis and Ruth B. Waxman (1973). Eliezer Berkovits, *Faith after the Holocaust* (1973) and Arthur A. Cohen, *Arguments and Doctrines: A Reader of Jewish Thinking in the Aftermath of the Holocaust* (1970), suggest additional perspectives.

Abrahams, Israel. *Jewish Life in the Middle Ages.* Philadelphia: Jewish Publication Soc., 1896. Repr.: New York: Meridian Books, 1958.

Altmann, Alexander. *Moses Mendelssohn: A Biographical Study.* University, Ala.: Univ. of Alabama Pr., 1973.

————, ed. *Studies in Nineteenth-Century Jewish Intellectual History.* Cambridge, Mass.: Harvard Univ. Pr., 1964.

Anti-Defamation League of B'nai B'rith. *The Study of Judaism: Bibliographical Essays.* New York: KTAV, 1972.

Baer, Yitzhak. *A History of the Jews in Christian Spain.* Tr. by Louis Schaffman. Philadelphia: Jewish Publication Soc., 1961–66. 2v.

Baron, Salo. *The Jewish Community.* Philadelphia: Jewish Publication Soc., 1942.

————. *The Russian Jew under Tsars and Soviets.* New York: Macmillan, 1964.

————. *A Social and Religious History of the Jews.* 2d ed. New York: Columbia Univ. Pr., 1952– . (Earlier, shorter version, 1937.)

Berkovits, Eliezer. *Faith after the Holocaust.* New York: KTAV, 1973.

Blau, Joseph L. *Judaism in America: From Curiosity to Third Faith.* Chicago: Univ. of Chicago Pr., 1976.

————. *Reform Judaism.* New York: KTAV, 1973.

Buber, Martin. *Eclipse of God.* New York: Harper & Row, 1952.

————. *I and Thou.* 2d ed. New York: Scribner's, 1958.

————. *Israel and the World.* New York: Schocken Books, 1948.

————. *On Judaism.* Ed. by N. N. Glatzer. New York: Schocken Books, 1967.

————. *The Origin and Meaning of Hasidism.* Ed. and tr. by M. Freedman. New York: Harper & Row, 1966.

————. *Tales of the Hasidim.* New York: Schocken Books, 1947–48. 2v.

Casper, Bernard M. *An Introduction to Jewish Bible Commentary.* New York: Thomas Yoseloff, 1960.

Cohen, Arthur A. *Arguments and Doctrines: A Reader of Jewish Thinking in the Aftermath of the Holocaust.* New York: Harper & Row, 1970.

Davidowicz, Lucy. *The Golden Tradition.* New York: Holt, Rinehart & Winston, 1967.

Davis, Moshe. *The Emergence of Conservative Judaism: The Historical School in 19th Century America.* Philadelphia: Jewish Publication Soc., 1963.

Diamond, Malcolm L. *Martin Buber, Jewish Existentialist.* New York: Oxford Univ. Pr., 1960.

Epstein, Isidore. *Judaism: A Historical Presentation.* London: Penguin, 1959.

Epstein, Louis M. *Sex Laws and Customs in Judaism.* New York: Bloch, 1948.

Flannery, Edward H. *The Anguish of the Jews: Twenty-three Centuries of Anti-Semitism.* New York: Macmillan, 1965.

Freehof, Solomon B. *The Response Literature.* Philadelphia: Jewish Publication Soc., 1955.

Friedman, Maurice. *Martin Buber: The Life of Dialogue.* Chicago: Univ. of Chicago Pr., 1955.

Gaster, Theodore H. *Customs and Folkways of Jewish Life.* New York: Sloane, 1955.

————. *Festivals of the Jewish Year.* New York: Manor, 1953, 1972.

————. *The Holy and the Profane: Evolution of Jewish Folkways.* New York: Sloane Assoc., 1955.

Ginsberg, Louis. *On Jewish Law and Lore.* Philadelphia: Jewish Publication Soc., 1955.

Glatzer, N. N. *A Jewish Reader: In Time and Eternity.* 2d ed. New York: Schocken Books, 1961.

————. *Franz Rosenzweig: His Life and Thought.* New York: Farrar, Straus & Young, 1953.

————, comp. *Language of Faith.* New York: Schocken Books, 1967.

————, ed. *The Dynamics of Emancipation.* Boston: Beacon Pr., 1965.

————, ed. *On Judaism, Martin Buber.* New York: Schocken Books, 1972.

————, ed. *On the Bible.* New York: Schocken Books, 1968.

Glazer, Nathan. *American Judaism.* 2d ed. Chicago: Univ. of Chicago Pr., 1972.

Goitein, S. D. *Jews and Arabs: Their Contacts through the Ages.* New York: Schocken Books, 1964.

Gordis, Robert, and Ruth B. Waxman, eds. *Faith and Reason: Essays in Judaism*. New York: KTAV, 1973.

Greenstone, Julius H. *The Messiah Idea in Jewish History*. Philadelphia: Jewish Publication Soc., 1906.

Hertzberg, Arthur. *The French Enlightenment and the Jews*. New York: Columbia Univ. Pr., 1968.

————. *Judaism*. New York: G. Braziller, 1961.

————, ed. *The Zionist Idea*. New York: Atheneum, 1972.

Kaplan, Mordecai. *Judaism as a Civilization*. New York: Schocken Books, 1967.

Kisch, Guido. *The Jews in Medieval Germany*. New York: KTAV, 1970.

Mahler, Raphael. *Jewish Emancipation*. New York: American Jewish Comm., 1941.

Mendelssohn, Moses. *Jerusalem and Other Jewish Writings*. Tr. and ed. by Alfred Jospe. New York: Schocken Books, 1969.

Meyer, Michael A. *The Origins of the Modern Jew: Jewish Identity and European Culture in Germany, 1749–1824*. Detroit: Wayne State Univ. Pr., 1967.

Millgram, Abraham E. *Jewish Worship*. Philadelphia: Jewish Publication Soc., 1971.

————, ed. *An Anthology of Medieval Hebrew Literature*. New York: Abelard-Schuman, 1961.

Mintz, Jerome R. *Legends of the Hasidim*. Chicago: Univ. of Chicago Pr., 1968.

Mueller, Ernst. *History of Jewish Mysticism*. Oxford: Phaedon Pr., 1946.

Neusner, Jacob. *The Way of Torah: An Introduction to Judaism*. Belmont, Calif.: Dickenson, 1970.

Newman, Louis I., tr. and ed. *The Hasidic Anthology*. New York: Schocken Books, 1963.

Parkes, James. *The Conflict of the Church and the Synagogue*. Philadelphia: Jewish Publication Soc., 1961.

————. *The Jew in the Medieval Community*. London: Soncino Pr., 1938.

————. *Judaism and Christianity*. Chicago: Univ. of Chicago Pr., 1948.

Philipson, David. *The Reform Movement in Judaism*. Rev. ed. New York: Macmillan, 1931.

Poliakov, Leon. *The History of Anti-Semitism*. New York: Vanguard, 1965–Vols. 1– .

Poll, Solomon. *The Hasidic Community of Williamsburg*. Glencoe, Ill.: Free Pr., 1962.

Rosenzweig, Franz. *The Star of Redemption*. Tr. by W. N. Halo. New York: Holt, Rinehart, 1971.

Roth, Cecil. *A History of the Jews in England*. Oxford: Clarendon Pr., 1949.

————. *The History of the Jews of Italy*. Philadelphia: Jewish Publication Soc., 1946.

————. *A History of the Marranos*. Philadelphia: Jewish Publication Soc., 1941.

————. *The Jews in the Renaissance*. Philadelphia: Jewish Publication Soc., 1959.

Samuel, Maurice. *The World of Sholom Aleichem*. New York: Knopf, 1943.

Sarachek, Joseph. *The Doctrine of the Messiah in Medieval Jewish Literature.* 2d ed. New York: Herman Pr., 1968.

Scholem, Gershom. *Kabbalah.* New York: Quadrangle, 1974.

———. *Major Trends in Jewish Mysticism.* New York: Schocken Books, 1941.

———. *The Messianic Idea in Judaism.* New York: Schocken Books, 1971.

———. *Sabbatai Sevi; The Mystical Messiah, 1626–1676.* Tr. by R. J. Warblowsky. Princeton, N.J.: Princeton Univ. Pr., 1973.

Schwartz, L. W., ed. *Great Ages and Ideas of the Jewish People.* New York: Random House, 1956.

Silver, Abba Hillel. *A History of Messianic Speculation in Israel.* Boston: Beacon Pr., 1959 (1927).

Sklare, Marshall. *America's Jews.* New York: Random House, 1971.

———. *Conservative Judaism.* New York: Schocken Books, 1972.

Stitskin, Leon D., ed. *Studies in Judaica.* New York: KTAV, 1974.

Trachtenberg, Joshua. *Jewish Magic and Superstition: A Study in Folk Religion.* New York: Behrman's, 1939.

HISTORICAL STUDY OF CHRISTIANITY IN MEDIEVAL AND MODERN TIMES

The systematic historical study of Christianity by North American scholars is a tradition conveniently symbolized by Philip Schaff. He immigrated to the United States in the 1840s as a German-trained scientific historian and theologian. Schaff began his career teaching at the Mercersburg Seminary before the American Civil War. Subsequently he was associated with the Union Theological Seminary in New York City. While there he compiled volumes that still have scholarly usefulness. In addition, he conceived a professional society dedicated to the study of Christian history, and was concurrently active in the founding years of the American Historical Association. The formative and early figures of the American Society of Church History have been traced into the twentieth century by Henry Warner Bowden in his *Church History in the Age of Science* (1971). Bowden makes much of the distinction between the criteria of scientific history writing and the various approaches of those who sought to study religious subjects in this era.

Scholarly interest within the society and its substantial journal, *Church History,* is primarily concerned with the late Medieval, Reformation, and modern periods, with special emphasis on Christianity in the English-speaking world. Yet an influence, traceable to Schaff, has assured some continuing attention to the full scope of Christian tradition. The society has also continued to have a more than incidental relationship to the American Historical Association in several areas. The members and participants in its programs and publications are not necessarily religious historians, but include many general historians who have specialized interests in the religious aspects of particular periods, figures, or traditions. In addition, the society continues to meet regularly with the American Historical Association and functions, in certain respects, as its specialized subsection on religion.

One consequence of this professional location and focus is that most of the contemporary historical work on Christianity, and Western religion in general, tends to be period specific. Few contemporary scholars venture to control Christian history in its entirety, thus failing to emulate Schaff's tradition-comprehending publications. Comprehensive historical studies of the Church are available, but they tend to be basically interpretative and thus highly selective.

The historical study of Christianity has been reduced in scope for a number of reasons. One of the more immediate is the extraordinary growth of general historical work on Western societies, especially in the modern era. This is so much the case that a high degree of specialization is required to master available primary sources and the secondary studies in numbers of separate areas. Vast cognate literatures in numerous languages underlie relevant studies within general history. In addition, individual scholars who may have originated in a distinctive subtradition, such as particular Lutheran or Roman Catholic circles, tend to have selective interests in the broader tradition. Further, Christianity has manifested a rich variety in its elaboration under different cultural settings. The great ranges of faith and practice still claiming to be within the tradition are the overwhelming reality that confronts a historian. Of course, the manifest pluralism within contemporary Christianity also contradicts the premise that in earlier periods and across various epochs a coherence and pronounced identity might once have existed.

The internal plurality of great religious traditions has been taken for granted from the outset of serious religious study. But the degree of abstraction required, for example, to make one religion (Hinduism) out of the confusing welter of Indian practices, or one (or possibly two) tradition(s) from the complexities of Buddhism, has seemed less implausible than such an effort with respect to Christianity. There are strategies available, of course, to address this problem. One means to achieve a comprehensive interpretation of Christianity is to start from a definition that will permit such a construction; for instance, the kind of understanding of Christianity developed by Schleiermacher, commonly held to be the architect of its liberal tradition. In his understanding, Christianity was that religion in which everything was related to Jesus Christ as redeemer. A recent study is Richard R. Neibuhr, *Schleiermacher on Christ and Religion* (1964). Starting with this as a normative definition of Christianity, the theologically determined historian is in a position to develop an extensive overview of the whole of Christian history that can readily identify orthodox, and specify heretical, versions of the tradition. In this kind of framework, it is possible to point to the general development, and perhaps decline, of the Christian religion. It is equally obvious that this kind of definition subjects the historical interpretation of Christianity to a theological point of departure, thus rendering it a very particular kind of historiography.

A second means to approach a comprehensive history of Christianity is represented in the heroic attempt to be encompassing, usually on an institutional or doctrinal basis. Such enterprises have been undertaken recently, for instance in the work of Kenneth Latourette. Of course, this kind of approach necessarily undervalues familiarity with the relevant general scholarship on particular periods and may also be problematical with respect to the definition of Christianity in anything but self-referential terms.

An approach explicitly drawing on the history of religions perspectives has been sketched out and more recently published in completed form. In a presidential address to the American Society of Church History, William A. Clebsch boldly called for a new historical approach to Christianity as a religion. He proposed to take account of the difficulties just enumerated by identifying major epochs in terms of particular cultural situations, and then analyzing the specific forms of the Christian religion in terms of the paradigms that developed in the course of each. His assumption is that in the several coherent cultural periods there will be recognizable forms of the quest for redemption as promised through Christianity, and that particular symbols and agencies would be developed within each one to achieve the salvation promised in the tradition. In this sense he takes the ground proposed by the liberal theological tradition as a starting point, but he is also sensitive to various cultural matrices in a way that a strictly theological program would not be. Clebsch's program does represent the interfertilization between more strictly historical inquiries and the history of religions methods and approaches that have had their consistent application, as has been seen, to extra-

Western materials. His completed study represents an approach to a history of Christianity as a whole that is sensitive to some of the issues sketched in the above paragraphs.

If comprehensive historical studies of the Christian religion are very much less common now than in the past, for the reasons suggested above (among others), long-term historical studies of particular aspects or facets of the Christian tradition have not been lacking. For example, the field of the history of Christian doctrine represents a discrete aspect of the Christian tradition that in some sense is self-defined. Doctrines are established under church authority. It is therefore possible to chronicle, or even systematically interpret in fully historical settings, the development of specific Christian doctrines. At the present time, this classical subliterature within the broader literature of Christian historiography is represented by Jaroslav Pelikan's scholarship.

For reflections upon the historical study of Christianity, see Jerald C. Brauer (editor), *Impact of the Church upon Its Culture: Reappraisals of the History of Christianity* (1968). For overall Church historical surveys, the following may prove to be useful: Philip Schaff, *History of the Christian Church* (reprint, 1972–75). For a more recent and inclusive survey see *History of the Expansion of Christianity* by Kenneth Scott Latourette (1937–45). His one-volume survey is *A History of Christianity* (1953). A current series projects five volumes and carries the title *The Christian Centuries: A New History of the Catholic Church* (1964–); L. J. Rogier, R. Aubert, D. Knowles, and J. T. Ellis are editors. A standard one-volume survey by Williston Walker, *A History of the Christian Church,* was revised by C. C. Richardson, W. Pauck, and R. T. Handy (1970).

An earlier section discussed literature on Christianity in the first centuries of the common era. For the Middle Ages, the following surveys may be useful. William R. Cannon contributed his *History of Christianity in the Middle Ages: From the Fall of Rome to the Fall of Constantinople* (1960). An older, small volume by Margaret Deanesley remains useful as a synoptic study: *A History of the Medieval Church, 590–1500* (1959). Richard W. Southern, *The Making of the Middle Ages* (1953), is highly regarded; see also his *Western Society and the Church in the Middle Ages* (1970). Carl A. Volz, *The Church of the Middle Ages* (1970) may also be noted.

On the divergence of Eastern and Western churches, see Deno Geanakoplos, *Byzantine East and Latin West* (1966). Steven Runciman, *Eastern Schism* (1955) and *The Great Church in Captivity: A*

Study of the Patriarchate of Constantinople from the Eve of the Turkish Conquest to the Greek War of Independence (1968) are concerned with aspects of Eastern Christianity. See also Aziz S. Atiya, *A History of Eastern Christianity* (1968) and Alexander Schmemann, *Historical Road of Eastern Orthodoxy* (1963).

More specialized studies of particular topics are identified by their titles. Marjorie Nicolson has abridged the three volumes of H. C. Lea, *A History of the Inquisition of the Middle Ages* (1958). On heresy, see Gordon Leff, *Heresy in the Later Middle Ages* (1967), and W. L. Wakefield and A. P. Evans (editors), *Heresies of the High Middle Ages* (1969). Marjorie Reeves, in her *Influence of Prophecy in the Later Middle Ages* (1969), signals the high degree of interest in the Joachite Movement or the Spiritual Franciscans. Jean Guitton, *Great Heresies and Church Councils* (1965) and Lorenz Jaeger, *The Ecumenical Councils, the Church and Christendom* (1961) may be useful. For background, see Brian Tierney, *The Foundations of the Councilar Theory* (1955).

The emergence of the Bishop of Rome as leader of the Western Church was fundamental to Christianity in Europe. For discussions of the topic, see Paolo Brezzi, *The Papacy: Its Origins and Historical Evolution* (1958), Geoffrey Barraclough, *The Medieval Papacy* (1968), and Walter Ullmann, *A Short History of the Papacy in the Middle Ages* (1972). The Crusades are discussed in Steven Runciman's three-volume *A History of the Crusades* (1951–54); see also the portrayal by Zoé Oldenbourg in *The Crusades* (1966).

Medieval religious thought and doctrine are discussed in the second and third volumes of Frederick Copleston's *A History of Philosophy* (1950–53), in G. W. H. Lampe (editor), *The West from the Fathers to the Reformation* (1969), in Etienne Gilson, *History of Christian Philosophy in the Middle Ages* (1955), and in Gordon Leff, *Medieval Thought: St. Augustine to Ockham* (1958). For the late Middle Ages, see Heiko Oberman, *The Harvest of Medieval Theology: Gabriel Biel and Late Medieval Nominalism* (1963). The development of worship is a central subject; see Gregory Dix, *The Shape of the Liturgy* (1945), Massey H. Shepherd (editor), *Worship in Scripture and Tradition* (1963), and J. H. Strawley, *The Early History of Liturgy* (1947). Finally, mysticism has been important in Western Christianity; see W. R. Inge, *Christian Mysticism* (1933), K. E. Kirk, *The Vision of God* (1932), and Jean LeClercq, et al., *The Spirituality of the Middle Ages* (1968). Jean LeClercq, *Love of Learning and the Desire for God* (1961), David Knowles, *Christian*

Monasticism (1969), and H. B. Workman, *The Evolution of the Monastic Ideal* (1962) are general treatments of monasticism.

The division of European Christendom in the late medieval and early modern periods has generated a vast scholarly literature. For an overview, see V. H. H. Green, *Renaissance and Reformation* (1964) and Donald Weinstein (editor), *Renaissance and the Reformation, 1300–1600* (1965). Roland H. Bainton, *The Reformation of the Sixteenth Century* (1952) is a popular presentation. G. H. Williams, *Radical Reformation* (1962) presents the so-called left wing groups of reformers. For a sociological discussion of the period, see Guy E. Swanson, *Religion and Regime: A Sociological Account of the Reformation* (1967).

The background to the Protestant revolt is reviewed in Heiko Oberman, *Forerunners of the Reformation* (1966). There is a vast amount of literature on Martin Luther: See Jaroslav Pelikan, *Interpreters of Luther* (1968); A. G. Dickens, *Martin Luther and the Reformation* (1967); and Brian Tierney, et al., *Martin Luther* (1968). John Calvin, the French-Swiss reformer, is readily approached through François Wendel, *Calvin: The Origins and Development of His Religious Thought* (1963). On Calvinism, see John T. McNeill, *The History and Character of Calvinism* (1954). A. G. Dickens, in *The English Reformation* (1964), presents the complex English developments, while Gordon Donaldson summarizes corresponding events in that kingdom in his *The Scottish Reformation* (1960). Keith Thomas, *Religion and the Decline of Magic* (1971) is an enormously suggestive anthropological approach to religion and its changes, especially in England in the early modern period.

On the emergence of patterns of Christianity in modern Europe, the following studies may be useful: Joseph Lecler's two-volume *Toleration and the Reformation* (1960); Gerald Cragg, *The Church and the Age of Reason, 1648–1789* (1961); Kenneth Scott Latourette's five-volume *Christianity in a Revolutionary Age* (1958–62); and Martin E. Marty, *Protestantism: Its Churches and Cultures, Rituals and Doctrines, Yesterday and Today* (1972). On intellectual trends, see James C. Livingston, *Modern Christian Thought: From the Enlightenment to Vatican II* (1971). Specialized studies on English Christianity that are broadly useful include: Alan Simpson, *Puritanism in Old and New England* (1955); Horton M. Davies, five-volume *Worship and Theology in England* (1961–75); Owen Chadwick and Geoffrey F. Nuttall (editors), *From Uniformity to Unity, 1662–1962* (1962); and Owen Chadwick, *The Mind of the Oxford Movement* (1960).

Atiya, Aziz S. *A History of Eastern Christianity*. London: Methuen, 1968.

Bainton, Roland H. *The Reformation of the Sixteenth Century*. Boston: Beacon Pr., 1952.

Barraclough, Geoffrey. *The Medieval Papacy*. London: Thames & Hudson, 1968.

Bowden, Henry Warner. *Church History in the Age of Science*. Chapel Hill, N.C.: Univ. of North Carolina Pr., 1971.

Brauer, Jerald C., ed. *Impact of the Church upon Its Culture: Reappraisals of the History of Christianity*. Chicago: Univ. of Chicago Pr., 1968.

Brezzi, Paolo. *The Papacy: Its Origins and Historical Evolution*. Westminster, Md.: Newman, 1958.

Cannon, William R. *History of Christianity in the Middle Ages: From the Fall of Rome to the Fall of Constantinople*. New York: Abingdon Pr., 1960.

Chadwick, Owen. *The Mind of the Oxford Movement*. Stanford, Calif.: Stanford Univ. Pr., 1960.

———, and Geoffrey F. Nuttall, eds. *From Uniformity to Unity, 1662–1962*. London: S.P.C.K., 1962.

Clebsch, William A. *Christianity in European History*. New York: Oxford Univ. Pr., 1979.

Copleston, Frederick. *A History of Philosophy*. Vols. 2, 3. Westminster, Md.: Newman, 1950–53.

Cragg, Gerald. *The Church and the Age of Reason, 1648–1789*. New York: Atheneum, 1961.

Davies, Horton M. *Worship and Theology in England*. Princeton, N.J.: Princeton Univ. Pr., 1961–75. 5v.

Deanesley, Margaret. *A History of the Medieval Church, 590–1500*. London: Methuen, 1959.

Dickens, A. G. *The English Reformation*. New York: Schocken Books, 1964.

———. *Martin Luther and the Reformation*. London: E.U.P., 1967.

Dix, Gregory. *The Shape of the Liturgy*. London: Dacre Pr., 1945.

Donaldson, Gordon. *The Scottish Reformation*. Cambridge: Cambridge Univ. Pr., 1960.

Geanakoplos, Deno. *Byzantine East and Latin West*. New York: Barnes & Noble, 1966.

Gilson, Etienne. *History of Christian Philosophy in the Middle Ages*. New York: Random House, 1955.

Green, V. H. H. *Renaissance and Reformation*. 2d ed. New York: St. Martin's Pr., 1964.

Guitton, Jean. *Great Heresies and Church Councils*. Tr. by F. D. Wieck. New York: Harper & Row, 1965.

Inge, W. R. *Christian Mysticism*. 7th ed. New York: Scribner's, 1933.

Jaeger, Lorenz. *The Ecumenical Councils, the Church and Christendom*. Tr. by A. V. Luthdale. New York: Kenedy, 1961.

Kirk, K. E. *The Vision of God*. 2d ed. New York: Longmans, Green, 1932.

Knowles, David. *Christian Monasticism*. London: Weidenfeld & Nicolson, 1969.

Lampe, G. W. H., ed. *The West from the Fathers to the Reformation*. New York: Cambridge Univ. Pr., 1969.

Latourette, Kenneth Scott. *Christianity in a Revolutionary Age: A History of Christianity in the Nineteenth and Twentieth Centuries.* New York: Harper & Row, 1958–62. 5v.

————. *A History of Christianity.* New York: Harper & Row, 1953.

————. *A History of the Expansion of Christianity.* New York: Harper & Row, 1937–45. 7v.

Lea, H. C. *A History of the Inquisition of the Middle Ages.* New York: Russell & Russell, 1958.

————. *The Inquisition of the Middle Ages.* Abridged by Marjorie Nicolson. New York: Macmillan, 1961.

Lecler, Joseph. *Toleration and the Reformation.* New York: Association Pr., 1960. 2v.

Leclercq, Jean. *The Love of Learning and the Desire for God.* New York: Fordham, 1961.

————, et al. *The Spirituality of the Middle Ages.* New York: Desclé, 1968.

Leff, Gordon. *Heresy in the Later Middle Ages.* Manchester: Manchester Univ. Pr., 1967.

————. *Medieval Thought: St. Augustine to Ockham.* Chicago: Quadrangle, 1958.

Livingston, James C. *Modern Christian Thought: From the Enlightenment to Vatican II.* New York: Macmillan, 1971.

Marty, Martin E. *Protestantism: Its Churches and Cultures, Rituals and Doctrines, Yesterday and Today.* New York: Holt, Rinehart & Winston, 1972.

McNeill, John T. *The History and Character of Calvinism.* New York: Oxford Univ. Pr., 1954.

Niebuhr, Richard R. *Schleiermacher on Christ and Religion.* New York: Scribner's, 1964.

Oberman, Heiko. *Forerunners of the Reformation.* New York: Holt, Rinehart & Winston, 1966.

————. *The Harvest of Medieval Theology: Gabriel Biel and Late Medieval Nominalism.* Cambridge, Mass.: Harvard Univ. Pr., 1963.

Oldenbourg, Zoé. *The Crusades.* New York: Pantheon, 1966.

Pelikan, Jaroslav. *Interpreters of Luther.* Philadelphia: Fortress, 1968.

Reeves, Marjorie. *The Influence of Prophecy in the Later Middle Ages.* Oxford: Clarendon Pr., 1969.

Rogier, L. J.; R. Aubert; D. Knowles; and J. T. Ellis, eds. *The Christian Centuries: A New History of the Catholic Church.* New York: McGraw-Hill, 1964– .

Runciman, Steven. *The Eastern Schism.* New York: Oxford Univ. Pr., 1955.

————. *The Great Church in Captivity: A Study of the Patriarchate of Constantinople from the Eve of the Turkish Conquest to the Greek War of Independence.* New York: Columbia Univ. Pr., 1968.

————. *A History of the Crusades.* Cambridge: Cambridge Univ. Pr., 1951–54. 3v.

Schaff, Philip. *History of the Christian Church.* (1889.) Repr.: Grand Rapids, Mich.: Eerdmans, 1972–75. 8v.

Schmemann, Alexander. *The Historical Road of Eastern Orthodoxy.* Tr. by Lydia Kesich. New York: Holt, 1963.

Shepherd, Massey ·H., ed. *Worship in Scripture and Tradition*. New York: Oxford Univ. Pr., 1963.

Simpson, Alan. *Puritanism in Old and New England*. Chicago: Univ. of Chicago Pr., 1955.

Southern, Richard W. *The Making of the Middle Ages*. New Haven, Conn.: Yale Univ. Pr., 1953.

——. *Western Society and the Church in the Middle Ages*. Harmondsworth, England: Penguin, 1970.

Strawley, J. H. *The Early History of Liturgy*. 2d ed. Cambridge: Cambridge Univ. Pr., 1947.

Swanson, Guy E. *Religion and Regime: A Sociological Account of the Reformation*. Ann Arbor: Univ. of Michigan Pr., 1967.

Thomas, Keith. *Religion and the Decline of Magic*. New York: Scribner's, 1971.

Tierney, Brian. *Foundations of the Councilar Theory*. Cambridge: Cambridge Univ. Pr., 1955.

——, et al. *Martin Luther*. New York: Random House, 1968.

Ullmann, Walter. *A Short History of the Papacy in the Middle Ages*. London: Methuen, 1972.

Volz, Carl A. *The Church of the Middle Ages*. St. Louis: Concordia, 1970.

Wakefield, W. L., and A. P. Evans, eds. *Heresies of the High Middle Ages*. New York: Columbia Univ. Pr., 1969.

Walker, Williston. *A History of the Christian Church*. Rev. by C. C. Richardson, W. Pauck, and R. T. Handy. New York: Scribner's, 1970.

Weinstein, Donald, ed. *The Renaissance and the Reformation, 1300–1600*. New York: Free Pr., 1965.

Wendel, François. *Calvin: The Origins and Development of His Religious Thought*. Tr. by Philip Mairet. London: Colliers, 1963.

Williams, G. H. *The Radical Reformation*. Philadelphia: Westminster Pr., 1962.

Workman, H. B. *The Evolution of the Monastic Ideal*. Boston: Beacon Pr., 1962.

AMERICAN RELIGIOUS HISTORY

The characteristics noted in the historical study of Christianity are even more pronounced when reviewing the history of religions, including Christianity, in North America. Several prominent traits include: (1) the significant decline of church historical interests; (2) a concentration upon religious subjects as securely anchored in frameworks shared with other cultural studies; (3) a coincidence of specialized religious historiography with the more generalized writings of cultural historians; and (4) an explicit appropriation of concepts, models, and explanatory mechanisms first developed in the social sciences. These characteristics can be observed at first hand in a collection of recent essays by John M. Mulder and John F. Wilson (editors) entitled *Religion in American History: Interpretative Essays* (1978). Because of the richness and vitality of recent work in this field, attention will first be given to general discussions and then to specific periods and topics.

Philip Schaff, whose name has been introduced as the founder of the critical historical study of Christianity in the United States, in the late nineteenth century sponsored a series of monographs on separate American denominational traditions. His principle of organization was based on attention to separate institutions with only one volume of thirteen devoted to a comprehensive discussion. It is an index of the changes in religious scholarship to note that the current summary volume by Sydney Ahlstrom carries the title *A Religious History of the American People* (1972). And yet, in another sense, synoptic volumes like Ahlstrom's, which posit religion rather than specific church traditions as their subject matter, continue to follow Schaff's emphasis on the denominational bodies as the primary institutional expressions and effective carriers of religious impulses within the society. The standard accounts all chart a basically linear pattern of religious transformation through American history from dominant Protestant groups to a pervasive pluralism. This same deep pattern may also be observed in a recent study by Robert T. Handy, which uses North America as the explicit subject; see his *A History of the Churches in the United States and Canada* (1977). Recent additions to this survey literature do challenge these assumptions; see Catherine Albanese, *America: Religion and Religions* (1981), and Peter Williams's discussion of *Popular Religion in America* (1980).

Monographs on particular aspects of American religion generally take for granted the same overall pattern. As examples, see William Clebsch, *From Sacred to Profane America* (1968) and Edwin Scott Gaustad, *Dissent in American Religion* (1973). While in a manifest sense histories of the Roman Catholic community in America tell a different story, that of its development from persecuted minority to an equal or majority partner in a pluralistic setting, the linear pattern is presupposed as background. In this sense the more innovative and important scholarly studies of American religion, like those of Christianity generally, tend to be period or subject specific.

Ahlstrom, Sydney. *A Religious History of the American People.* New Haven, Conn.: Yale Univ. Pr., 1972.
Albanese, Catherine. *America: Religion and Religions.* Belmont, Calif.: Wadsworth, 1981.

Clebsch, William. *American Religious Thought: A History*. Chicago: Univ. of Chicago Pr., 1973.

———. *From Sacred to Profane America*. New York: Harper & Row, 1968.

Gaustad, Edwin S. *Dissent in American Religion*. Chicago: Univ. of Chicago Pr., 1973.

Handy, Robert T. *A History of the Churches in the United States and Canada*. New York: Oxford Univ. Pr., 1977.

Mulder, John M., and John F. Wilson, eds. *Religion in American History: Interpretive Essays*. Englewood Cliffs, N.J.: Prentice-Hall, 1978.

Strout, Cushing. *The New Heavens and New Earth: Political Religion in America*. New York: Harper & Row, 1974.

Williams, Peter. *Popular Religion in America: Symbolic Change and the Modernization Process*. Englewood Cliffs, N.J.: Prentice-Hall, 1980.

New England Puritanism

Perry Miller made his scholarly province the interpretation of Puritanism as the point of origin for American culture. As professor of history and literature at Harvard, Miller's major studies include *The New England Mind: The Seventeenth Century* (1939), a magisterial analysis of the cosmos as rendered theologically intelligible through transmutation of Calvinism, and *The New England Mind: From Colony to Province* (1953), which reviewed the basic transformations of the original social and intellectual impulse through the first several generations. Additional essays and studies of separate figures (especially Roger Williams and Jonathan Edwards) and discrete essays created a synthetic interpretation of the first 150 years of New England culture that has exercised fascination over several generations of younger scholars. Numerous studies, some under Miller's guidance but many less directly indebted to him, have explored these religious and cultural materials. The effect has been to refine his synthesis at points and to propose new interpretations at others. But the important consideration is that Miller effectively became a religious historian of New England culture. The agenda left to his heirs has been explored with equal vigor by historians, students of literature, and religious scholars.

Among the most significant studies since Miller's time have been several by Edmund Morgan, including *Visible Saints* (1963) and his study of John Winthrop in *The Puritan Dilemma* (1958). Attention should also be called to David D. Hall, *The Faithful Shepherd* (1972), Richard L. Bushman, *From Puritan to Yankee* (1970), Edwin S. Gaustad, *The Great Awakening in New England* (1957), William McLoughlin, *New England Dissent, 1630–1833* (1971), and E. Brooks Holifield, *The Covenant Sealed* (1974)—among many other monographs. A recent study by Philip Greven, entitled *The Protestant Temperament* (1977), analyzes connections between religious patterns of child rearing and social attitudes and actions in the culture, while David E. Stannard in *The Puritan Way of Death* (1977) uses that subject as a lens through which to view the culture. For studies of literary interests, see especially the recent work by Sacvan Bercovitch, *The Puritan Origins of the American Self* (1975) and *The American Jeremiad* (1978). Together with Emory Elliott, *Power and the Pulpit in Puritan New England* (1975) and Mason I. Lowance, Jr., *The Language of Canaan* (1980), they show the continuing attention given to religious subjects by students of early American literature. Included among current projects indebted to the impetus initiated by Perry Miller is a critical edition of Jonathan Edwards's writings, to include many unpublished as well as new editions of previously published works.

This literature, and numerous other studies not cited, clearly show that specific studies of church history tend to dissolve into cultural studies with a religious focus. Genuine interdisciplinary scholarship encompasses the work of social and literary historians and historians of religion, to name only the obvious contributors.

Puritanism, as the central emphasis of New England culture from the settlements on the Atlantic coast in the early seventeenth century to the Great Awakening in the middle of the eighteenth century, has received extraordinary attention from scholars representing a range of disciplines. This condition has not been paralleled for the other regions of settlement. The Southern colonies were more religiously coherent in allegiance to the Church of England, and also more exclusively British in ethnic terms. Interdisciplinary studies of Virginia, Maryland, and the Carolinas, comparable to those available in such numbers for New England, are needed—although recent article literature, especially in the *William and Mary Quarterly,* suggests that such studies will be developed. As for the middle colonies, the inherent ethnic and religious pluralism of the region, including Dutch, English, Scottish, Swedish, and German settlers, among others, invites studies that depart from an analysis of the religious pluralism of contemporary American life. Perhaps more than any other colony outside New England, Pennsylvania has been favored with balanced studies of the type already indicated for the Northern region. See especially Frederick Tolles, *Meeting House and Counting House* (1948), Mary Maples Dunn, *William Penn: Politics and Con-*

science (1967), and Melvin Endy, *William Penn and Early Quakerism* (1973).

To this point scholarship on other aspects of early American religious life has not received comparable attention. Especially the religious aspects of the Spanish Conquest and colonization and the efforts with respect to New France require additional work. Study of interaction between European settlers and the native Americans, however, now seems to be underway, as noted later in this essay.

Bercovitch, Sacvan. *The American Jeremiad.* Madison: Univ. of Wisconsin Pr., 1978.

———. *The Puritan Origins of the American Self.* New Haven, Conn.: Yale Univ. Pr., 1975.

Bushman, Richard L. *From Puritan to Yankee.* Cambridge, Mass.: Harvard Univ. Pr., 1967; New York: Norton, 1970.

Dunn, Mary Maples. *William Penn: Politics and Conscience.* Princeton, N.J.: Princeton Univ. Pr., 1967.

Elliott, Emory. *Power and the Pulpit in Puritan New England.* Princeton, N.J.: Princeton Univ. Pr., 1975.

Endy, Melvin. *William Penn and Early Quakerism.* Princeton, N.J.: Princeton Univ. Pr., 1973.

Gaustad, Edwin S. *The Great Awakening in New England.* New York: Harper & Row, 1957.

Greven, Philip. *The Protestant Temperament.* New York: Knopf, 1977.

Hall, David D. *The Faithful Shepherd: A History of the New England Ministry in the Seventeenth Century.* Chapel Hill: Univ. of North Carolina Pr., 1972.

Holifield, E. Brooks. *The Covenant Sealed.* New Haven, Conn.: Yale Univ. Pr., 1974.

Lowance, Mason I., Jr. *The Language of Canaan.* Cambridge, Mass.: Harvard Univ. Pr., 1980.

McLoughlin, William. *New England Dissent, 1630–1833.* Cambridge, Mass.: Harvard Univ. Pr., 1971. 2v.

Miller, Perry. *The New England Mind: From Colony to Province.* Cambridge, Mass.: Harvard Univ. Pr., 1953.

———. *The New England Mind: The Seventeenth Century.* Cambridge, Mass.: Harvard Univ. Pr., 1939.

Morgan, Edmund. *The Puritan Dilemma: The Story of John Winthrop.* Boston: Little, Brown, 1958.

———. *Visible Saints: The History of a Puritan Idea.* New York: New York Univ. Pr., 1963.

Stannard, David E. *The Puritan Way of Death: A Study in Religion, Culture and Social Change.* New York: Oxford Univ. Pr., 1977.

Tolles, Frederick. *Meeting House and Counting House.* Chapel Hill: Univ. of North Carolina Pr., 1948.

The National Period

For several decades, the period of the American Revolution remained essentially untouched by the kind of sensitive analysis that had explored colonial New England in such a way as to highlight its religious dimensions. Recently this defect seems to have been repaired. In particular, the celebration of the bicentennial of the nation's independence launched numerous projects. A more substantial factor may have been the recovery of appreciation for an ideological aspect of the struggle that raised anew the question of the role played by religious ideas and institutions in the conflict with England. Bernard Bailyn's *Ideological Origins of the American Revolution* (1967) made evident the importance of Whig ideas to the American struggle. In a counterposition, Alan Heimert in his *Religion and the American Mind* (1966) vigorously argued for the importance of evangelicalism as the mainspring of the Revolutionary effort. Most recently, Catherine L. Albanese has provided a stimulating analysis of the religiously generative aspects of the Revolutionary epoch; see *Sons of the Fathers: The Civil Religion of the American Revolution* (1976). Nathan Hatch's analysis of civil millenarianism in Revolutionary and post-Revolutionary preaching has further contributed to appreciation for the religious aspects of the founding of the new nation: see *The Sacred Cause of Liberty: Republican Thought and the Millennium in Revolutionary New England* (1977).

Scholarship concerned with the national period of American history manifests a significant interest in religious figures, movements, and issues, and it may be most useful to report it on an essentially topical basis. One topic, involving the emergence of revivalism as a deep cultural pattern, has received attention for some years. An older comprehensive discussion that brings the story down to Billy Graham is William G. McLoughlin's *Modern Revivalism* (1959). Timothy L. Smith persuasively argued that interest in another world did not render revival figures disinterested in this one in his *Revivalism and Social Reform* (1957). The energies set loose by revivalism issued in a complex of benevolence and reform societies. For a different point of view, see Clifford S. Griffin, *Their Brothers' Keepers* (1960), which discusses the effort as the work of moral busybodies. Charles I. Foster, *An Errand of Mercy* (1960) analyzes much the same effort as a conservative response to the French Revolution. Bertram Wyatt-Brown, *Lewis Tappan and the Evangelical War against Slavery* (1969) discusses an important lay leader of the movement. The importance of religion in the developing sectional struggle is brought to focus in Donald G. Mathews, *Religion in the Old South* (1977). For a discussion of prominent Southern theologians, see E. Brooks Holifield, *The Gentlemen Theologians* (1978).

Whitney R. Cross studied the religiously expressed ferment of the early national period as concentrated in upper New York State in his *The Burned-over District* (1950). On the Shakers, Edward D. Andrews provides a good overall discussion in his *People Called Shakers* (1953). For Joseph Smith, Jr., prophet and founder of the Mormon movement, see Fawn M. Brodie, *No Man Knows My History: The Life of Joseph Smith* (1971). A comprehensive discussion of the history of the Mormons written by Leonard J. Arrington and Davis Bitton is *The Mormon Experience: A History of the Latter-day Saints* (1979). John Humphrey Noyes founded the Oneida Community as an expression of communitarian socialism; see Maren L. Carden, *Oneida: Utopian Community to Modern Corporation* (1969).

The association of Protestantism with long-term cultural development has been studied in several perspectives. Ernest L. Tuveson, *Redeemer Nation* (1968) explores millenarian themes and their variants. Both Robert T. Handy, *A Christian America* (1971), and Martin E. Marty, *The Righteous Empire* (1970), review the conjunction between the national identity and Protestant self-consciousness. The discussion by T. Scott Miyakawa, *Protestants and Pioneers* (1964) is very suggestive of the problems involved in the opening of the West. The exploration of new religious symbols and other traditions as sources for American culture may be seen in Catherine L. Albanese, *Corresponding Motion: Transcendental Religion and the New America* (1977), a study of the Transcendentalist party. On the religious connections of the latter, see William R. Hutchison, *The Transcendentalist Ministers* (1959).

Given the reconstellation of American society under the impact of rapid industrialization following the Civil War, numerous changes took place in patterns of religious life. Robert Cross, *The Church and the City* (1967) offers a good cross-sectional introduction. A biographical study, *Dwight L. Moody, American Evangelist, 1837–1899*, by James F. Findlay, Jr. (1969), provides an additional means of approach to the era. A recent collaborative study of the so-called social gospel by C. Howard Hopkins and Ronald White suggests the several dimensions and ramifications of that impulse: *The Social Gospel: Religion and Reform in Changing America* (1976). A superb study by William R. Hutchison, *The Modernist Impulse in American Protestantism* (1976), is the best means to approach liberal Protestantism at the turn of the century. The counterposition is reviewed by Ernest R. Sandeen in his *The Roots of Fundamentalism: British and American Millenarianism, 1830–1900* (1970). Donald B. Meyer, *The Positive Thinkers* (1965) explores yet another facet of modern American culture of the late nineteenth and early twentieth centuries, the conjunction between concern for health, success, and happiness that often was expressed in a religious manner. In another study, *The Protestant Search for Political Realism, 1919–1941* (1960), Meyer reviews the political and social setting for the later "neo-orthodox" impulse, discussed under the portion of this essay dealing with religious thought.

Albanese, Catherine L. *Corresponding Motion: Transcendental Religion and the New America.* Philadelphia: Temple Univ. Pr., 1977.
———. *Sons of the Fathers: The Civil Religion of the American Revolution.* Philadelphia: Temple Univ. Pr., 1976.
Andrews, Edward D. *The People Called Shakers.* New York: Oxford Univ. Pr., 1953.
Arrington, Leonard J., and Davis Bitton. *The Mormon Experience: A History of the Latter-day Saints.* New York: Knopf, 1979.
Bailyn, Bernard. *Ideological Origins of the American Revolution.* Cambridge, Mass.: Harvard Univ. Pr., 1967.
Brodie, Fawn M. *No Man Knows My History: The Life of Joseph Smith.* New York: Knopf, 1971.
Carden, Maren L. *Oneida: Utopian Community to Modern Corporation.* Baltimore, Md.: Johns Hopkins Univ. Pr., 1969.
Cross, Robert. *The Church and the City, 1865–1910.* Indianapolis, Ind.: Bobbs-Merrill, 1967.
Cross, Whitney R. *The Burned-over District.* Ithaca, N.Y.: Cornell Univ. Pr., 1950.
Findlay, James F., Jr. *Dwight L. Moody: American Evangelist 1837–1899.* Chicago: Univ. of Chicago Pr., 1969.
Foster, Charles I. *An Errand of Mercy.* Chapel Hill: Univ. of North Carolina Pr., 1960.
Griffin, Clifford S. *Their Brothers' Keepers.* New Brunswick, N.J.: Rutgers Univ. Pr., 1960.
Handy, Robert T. *A Christian America.* New York: Oxford Univ. Pr., 1971.
Hatch, Nathan. *The Sacred Cause of Liberty: Republican Thought and the Millennium in Revolutionary New England.* New Haven, Conn.: Yale Univ. Pr., 1977.
Heimert, Alan. *Religion and the American Mind.* Cambridge, Mass.: Harvard Univ. Pr., 1966.
Holifield, E. Brooks. *The Gentlemen Theologians: American Theology in Southern Culture, 1795–1860.* Durham, N.C.: Duke Univ. Pr., 1978.

Hopkins, C. Howard, and Ronald White. *The Social Gospel: Religion and Reform in Changing America*. Philadelphia: Temple Univ. Pr., 1976.

Hutchison, William R. *The Modernist Impulse in American Protestantism*. Cambridge, Mass.: Harvard Univ. Pr., 1976.

————. *The Transcendentalist Ministers*. New Haven, Conn.: Yale Univ. Pr., 1959.

Marty, Martin E. *Righteous Empire*. New York: Dial, 1970.

Mathews, Donald G. *Religion in the Old South*. Chicago: Univ. of Chicago Pr., 1977.

McLoughlin, William G. *Modern Revivalism*. New York: Ronald Pr., 1959.

Meyer, Donald B. *The Positive Thinkers*. Garden City, N.Y.: Doubleday, 1965.

————. *The Protestant Search for Political Realism, 1919–1941*. Berkeley: Univ. of California Pr., 1960.

Miyakawa, T. Scott. *Protestants and Pioneers*. Chicago: Univ. of Chicago Pr., 1964.

Sandeen, Ernest R. *The Roots of Fundamentalism: British and American Millenarianism, 1830–1900*. Chicago: Univ. of Chicago Pr., 1970.

Smith, Timothy L. *Revivalism and Social Reform*. New York: Abingdon Pr., 1957.

Tuveson, Ernest L. *Redeemer Nation: The Idea of America's Millennial Role*. Chicago: Univ. of Chicago Pr., 1968.

Wyatt-Brown, Bertram. *Lewis Tappan and the Evangelical War against Slavery*. Cleveland, Ohio: Press of C.W.R.U., 1969.

New Fields of Critical Scholarship

Some studies of Jewish religious life in America have been discussed earlier in this chapter. The first fruits of important critical scholarship on the American Catholic community are now available. Notable studies of the indicated subjects include: Philip Gleason, *The Conservative Reformers: German-American Catholics and the Social Order* (1968); Jay P. Dolan, *The Immigrant Church: New York's Irish and German Catholics, 1815–1865* (1975) and *Catholic Revivalism: The American Experience, 1830–1900* (1978); Robert D. Cross, *The Emergence of Liberal Catholicism in America* (1967); and Harold J. Abramson, *Ethnic Diversity in Catholic America* (1973). A fascinating literature provides reflections by intellectuals upon the drastic changes in the American Roman Catholic Church and its community in recent years; for good examples, see Francine DuPlessix Gray, *Divine Disobedience* (1970) and Garry Wills, *Bare-ruined Choirs* (1972).

Recent scholarship has contributed to a fuller understanding of the significance of religious life among black Americans in a society newly conscious of deep racial divisions. E. Franklin Frazier's development of his Frazer Lecture, first published as *The Negro Church in*

America (1964), was reissued with a supplementary essay by C. Eric Lincoln entitled "The Black Church since Frazier" (1974). The subject of racial attitudes among white colonists is compellingly explored in Winthrop D. Jordan, *White over Black* (1968). Religious life within the slave community is studied by Albert J. Raboteau in *Slave Religion: The "Invisible Institution" in the Antebellum South* (1978). The cultural centrality of religious language and practice to slave society is presented in Eugene Genovese, *Roll, Jordan, Roll: The World the Slaves Made* (1974). This appreciation for the significance of religion in the history of the American black community renews perspectives advanced by W. E. B. DuBois early in the century. See especially his gentle essay *The Souls of Black Folks* (1903).

Cult movements among black Americans have frequently received attention because, migrating from the rural South, they have become so prominent in the northern urban industrial centers. Arthur Huff Fauset's *Black Gods of the Metropolis* (1944) was an early study. The most colorful figure was probably Father Divine—see Sara Harris's book by that title (1971). C. Eric Lincoln studied the Black Muslims as they began to achieve prominence: see his *The Black Muslims in America* (1961). For a different perspective on the same movement, see *Black Nationalism* (1962) by E. U. Essien-Udom. The *Autobiography of Malcolm X* (1965) by Malcolm Little is a remarkable introduction not only to the Muslim movement but to the range of religious life within the black community during the middle decades of the twentieth century.

Scholarly concern with women as religious subjects is beginning to develop as a self-conscious field. For a recent study concerned with gender differentiation in religious sensibility, see Amanda Porterfield, *Feminine Spirituality in America: From Sarah Edwards to Martha Graham* (1980). The influence of women's religious experience in transforming at least segments of the culture at large is the theme of *The Feminization of American Culture* (1977) by Ann Douglas.

Native American religions have been studied by anthropologists for many years. Scholars with specific interests in the history of religions are now beginning to turn to this subject. *Native American Religions* (1981) by Sam Gill is such a text. Religious aspects of cultural interaction between colonists and native Americans are explored in Henry W. Bowden, *American Indians and Christian Missions: Studies in Cultural Conflict* (1981).

The overall religious shape of American society has been a matter of interest at least since Will Herberg offered a stimulating thesis in his *Protestant-Catholic-Jew* (1955). For attempts at more recent characterization, see Andrew Greeley, *The Denominational Society* (1973) and Martin E. Marty, *A Nation of Behavers* (1976). Especially prominent in contemporary America, though scarcely unprecedented, are groups and movements inspired by Eastern religions or offering salvation in nontraditional terms. On these developments, see Jacob Needleman, *The New Religions* (1970). A substantial collection of essays edited by Irving Zaretsky and Mark P. Leone (editors), *Religious Movements in Contemporary America* (1974), brings together various perspectives on diverse religious groups.

Abramson, Harold J. *Ethnic Diversity in Catholic America.* New York: Wiley, 1973.

Bowden, Henry W. *American Indians and Christian Missions: Studies in Cultural Conflict.* Chicago: Univ. of Chicago Pr., 1981.

Cross, Robert D. *The Emergence of Liberal Catholicism in America.* Cambridge, Mass.: Harvard Univ. Pr., 1967.

Dolan, Jay P. *Catholic Revivalism: The American Experience, 1830–1900.* Notre Dame, Ind.: Univ. of Notre Dame Pr., 1978.

————. *The Immigrant Church: New York's Irish and German Catholics, 1815–1865.* Baltimore, Md.: Johns Hopkins Univ. Pr., 1975.

Douglas, Ann. *The Feminization of American Culture.* New York: Knopf, 1977.

DuBois, W. E. B. *The Souls of Black Folks.* Chicago: McClurg, 1903.

Essien-Udom, E. U. *Black Nationalism: A Search for Identity in America.* Chicago: Univ. of Chicago Pr., 1962.

Fauset, Arthur Huff. *Black Gods of the Metropolis: Negro Religious Cults in the Urban North.* Philadelphia: Univ. of Pennsylvania Pr., 1944.

Frazier, E. Franklin. *The Negro Church in America.* New York: Schocken Books, 1964.

————, and C. Eric Lincoln. *The Negro Church in America* and *The Black Church since Frazier.* New York, Schocken Books, 1974.

Genovese, Eugene. *Roll, Jordan, Roll: The World the Slaves Made.* New York: Pantheon, 1974.

Gill, Sam. *Native American Religions.* Belmont, Calif.: Wadsworth, 1981.

Gleason, Philip. *The Conservative Reformers: German-American Catholics and the Social Order.* Notre Dame, Ind.: Univ. of Notre Dame Pr., 1968.

Gray, Francine DuPlessix. *Divine Disobedience.* New York: Knopf, 1970.

Greeley, Andrew. *The Denominational Society.* Glenview, Ill.: Scott, Foresman, 1973.

Harris, Sara. *Father Divine.* New York: Macmillan, 1971.

Herberg, Will. *Protestant-Catholic-Jew.* Garden City, N.Y.: Doubleday, 1955.

Jordan, Winthrop D. *White over Black.* Chapel Hill: Univ. of North Carolina Pr., 1968.

Lincoln, C. Eric. *The Black Muslims in America.* Boston: Beacon Pr., 1961.

Little, Malcolm. *The Autobiography of Malcolm X*. New York: Grove Pr., 1965.

Marty, Martin E. *A Nation of Behavers*. Chicago: Univ. of Chicago Pr., 1976.

Needleman, Jacob. *The New Religions*. Garden City, N.Y.: Doubleday, 1970.

Porterfield, Amanda. *Feminine Spirituality in America: From Sarah Edwards to Martha Graham*. Philadelphia: Temple Univ. Pr., 1980.

Raboteau, Albert J. *Slave Religion: The "Invisible Institution" in the Antebellum South*. New York: Oxford Univ. Pr., 1978.

Wills, Garry. *Bare-ruined Choirs*. Garden City, N.Y.: Doubleday, 1972.

Zaretsky, Irving, and Mark P. Leone, eds. *Religious Movements in Contemporary America*. Princeton, N.J.: Princeton Univ. Pr., 1974.

4

Religious Thought and Ethics

For reasons previously suggested, constructive religious thought has undergone deep shifts in recent decades. The general cultural development represented by the emergence of religion as a conceptualization for modern scholarly endeavors has directly affected the self-consciousness of those who speak for separate traditions. This new perspective on traditional patterns of belief (and behavior) was indicated at the beginning of this essay. So influential has it been upon intellectual life that it has worked to limit the scope or reference of constructive proposals within given traditions in several respects. On the one hand, religion identifies a differentiated aspect of culture, comparable to politics, art, and other conventionally recognized ranges of human cultural activity. Certainly in modernized societies, traditional religions do not provide a comprehensive ordering of life on a culture-wide basis—but play this role if at all only for individuals or discrete subcultures. On the other hand, religious thought as a way of thinking is separated from politics or art, as well as from consistently scientific ways of attempting to render the social world intelligible, such as psychology and sociology. One consequence of the development of autonomous scholarly traditions with secure institutional support has been to diminish the significance of traditional religious thought as a guide to individual and collective life. Both of these aspects of cultural development—explicit religious traditions as parts of culture rather than as dominant within the whole, and religious thought as one among other means to secure the intelligibility of life—have worked to severely reduce the scope, reach, or richness of constructive religious reflection in recent scholarship.

Another and related reason for the shift in traditional religious thought has been the pervasive influence of cultural relativism. The literature cited in the preceding sections represents the proliferation of studies about cultures in their religious variety and manifoldness. This has directly undermined the compellingness of the unique claims asserted and acted on by each. Knowing about religious symbols and rituals in such diverse cultural settings as that of the Eskimo, of tribal life in New Guinea, of traditional Indian society, and of life among Zen Buddhists, makes less plausible the high and absolute claims of traditional Western monotheisms—be it Israel's ancient belief in her choseness or assertions about a trinitarian Christian Godhead. On the other hand, when traditional formulas are interpreted as symbolic claims only, they are juxtaposed with other sets of religious symbols and are subject to interpretation in psychological and sociological frameworks, as are any other cultural symbols. In this perspective it is clear that in recent decades theology has been deeply affected by the same Enlightenment sources that influenced the conceptualization of religion.

PHILOSOPHICAL STUDY OF RELIGION

The cultural developments so described have led to at least two kinds of responses among philosophers interested in religious thought. One response has been a turning to broader philosophical or cultural criticism. This is one means to understand the particular situation of religious thought—which in principle ought not to be different from cognate aspects of culture. For example, the enormously influential proposal by Thomas Kuhn that the development of science, especially in the modern world, must be understood in terms of "paradigm shifts" has seemed directly relevant to interpretation of many kinds of cultural activities, including theology. See his *The Structure of Scientific Revolutions* (1970). Similarly, proposals concerning "interpretation" made by a figure like Paul Ricoeur have struck a responsive chord in much the same fashion. Recent publications by Bryan Wilson and Alasdair MacIntyre illustrate this type of philosophical response to modernity on the part of philosophers interested in religious thought. On this approach, religious thought in modern society is thought to be in fundamentally the same position as comparable cultural activities.

A second kind of response has been the application of more strictly philosophical resources of the analytical tradition (or linguistic philosophy) to review classical issues of religious thought, issues such as that of the traditional proofs for the existence of God. Scholarly discussion of these questions has been carried on within technical philosophical circles as well as among religious scholars. Frequently major contributions have first appeared in the form of journal articles, and only secondarily have they become circulated in collections of essays. An early and very influential set of essays was edited by Antony Flew and Alasdair MacIntyre. A comprehensive introduction to this second kind of response may be consulted in *Contemporary Philosophy and Religious Thought* by Malcolm L. Diamond (1974). The journal *Religious Studies* (1965–) is a medium for this kind of discussion.

Alston, William P., ed. *Religious Belief and Philosophical Thought*. New York: Harcourt, Brace, 1963.

Christian, William A. *Meaning and Truth in Religion*. Princeton, N.J.: Princeton Univ. Pr., 1964.

Diamond, Malcolm L. *Contemporary Philosophy and Religious Thought*. New York: McGraw-Hill, 1974.

Evans, Donald D. *The Logic of Self-Involvement*. London: SCM Press, 1963.

Ferre, Frederick. *Basic Modern Philosophy of Religion*. New York: Scribner's, 1967.

———. *Language, Logic and God*. New York: Harper & Row, 1961.

Flew, Antony, and Alasdair MacIntyre, eds. *New Essays in Philosophical Theology*. London: SCM Press, 1955.

Geach, Peter. *God and the Soul*. New York: Schocken Books, 1969.

Kenny, Anthony. *The Five Ways*. London: Routledge, 1969.

Kuhn, Thomas. *The Structure of Scientific Revolutions*. Chicago: Univ. of Chicago Pr., 1970.

Mavrodes, George I., ed. *The Rationality of Belief in God*. Englewood Cliffs, N.J.: Prentice-Hall, 1970.

Mitchell, Basil, ed. *Faith and Logic*. London: Allen & Unwin, 1957.

Plantinga, Alvin. *God and Other Minds*. Ithaca, N.Y.: Cornell Univ. Pr., 1967.

Preller, Victor. *Divine Science and the Science of God*. Princeton, N.J.: Princeton Univ. Pr., 1967.

Ricoeur, Paul. *The Conflict of Interpretations: Essays in Hermeneutics*. Ed. by Don Ihde. Evanston, Ill.: Northwestern Univ. Pr., 1974.

———. *History and Truth: Essays*. Evanston, Ill.: Northwestern Univ. Pr., 1965.

Ross, James F. *Introduction to the Philosophy of Religion*. New York: Macmillan, 1969.

Santani, Ronald E., ed. *Religious Language and the Problem of Religious Knowledge*. Bloomington, Ind.: Indiana Univ. Pr., 1968.

Smart, Ninian. *The Philosophy of Religion*. New York: Random House, 1970.

———. *Reasons and Faiths*. London: Routledge & Kegan Paul, 1959.

Wilson, Bryan R., ed. *Rationality*. Oxford: Blockwell, 1970.

CONSTRUCTIVE RELIGIOUS THOUGHT

The two kinds of philosophical interest in religious thought just discussed contrast sharply with the brilliant flowering of theology that occurred in the decades between the world wars. That episode included major restatements of comprehensive theological positions, often conforming to orthodox prescriptions. The best parallels to this flowering may lie in the High Middle Ages and the religious struggles of the sixteenth century. Karl Barth, Rudolf Bultmann, Paul Tillich and, especially in the United States, Reinhold and Richard Niebuhr, together with associates, constituted a galaxy of theological figures whose published works circulated widely and were discussed well beyond the confines of religious bodies and the circles associated with them. Comparable to these specifically Protestant thinkers were such Jewish figures as Martin Buber, previously cited, and Abraham Heschel. For the Roman Catholics, distinguished philosophers like Jacques Maritain and Etienne Gilson developed a renewed appreciation for the intellectual vitality and richness of the Christian tradition in the Middle Ages. In the decades of the most intensive theological discussion, the designation "neo-orthodoxy" was widely used—especially for the group of Protestant thinkers who appeared in a cultural framework as religious apologists. All were widely known, and particular figures were warmly received within political and academic circles. Their influence as intellectuals extended far beyond the conventional reach of religious thinkers in modern Western societies.

In retrospect, it is evident that these figures did not share any common point of view. In some, a predominant impetus came from Christian existentialist philosophy, especially mediated through Soren Kierkegaard. This philosophy was joined to a belief that, in the cultural crisis then being experienced by the West, the ancient religious traditions represented a philosophical anchor. But the versions of the tradition that were recovered in this way varied widely indeed. It may be well to suggest this range. At one extreme Karl Barth presented the assertion of a hyper-redemptionist view of history vis-à-vis the world. The scope of his vision and the range of his scholarly learning were breathtaking; he represented a very different perspective than that found in Reinhold Niebuhr's work. The latter agonized over questions of social justice and sought to make discriminating judgments about political issues. To this end he emphasized the utility of biblically derived religious symbols in comprehending what otherwise seemed to be an unintelligible social and political world. No less did this program differ from Rudolph Bultmann's proposal that the Christian message must be understood in terms of "demythologizing"—that is, separating the cultural influences imposed upon the self-understanding of the early movement, so as to identify the kernel or central truth of Christianity. Martin Buber's dialectical understanding of the Jewish tradition, and Jacques Maritain's recovery of appreciation for a rich and nuanced scholasticism, were also very particular and individual programs. What held them together was little more—but clearly no less—than the conviction that the ancient religious traditions of the West remained relevant to modern humanity.

When the manifoldness of the renaissance in religious thought at midcentury is recognized, it is not surprising that later generations moved off from this position in a great variety of directions. For instance, in the work of Harvey Cox the social idealism of the American tradition worked its way into a celebration of the secular city as the sphere of a redemption already achieved. For Paul Van Buren, the analytical program of linguistic philosophy moved him in a rigorously reductive direction in search of the meaning of the gospel. A somewhat comparable impulse, but dependent for its constructive side upon a general philosophical scheme derived from process philosophy, can be found in the work of Schubert Ogden, a contemporary very much influenced by Bultmann. Others, such as Gabriel Vahanian, explicitly welcomed and celebrated the "death of God," as the beginning of a modern liberation. Thus the generation succeeding the theological renaissance that ended at midcentury has carried through the pluralism of that renaissance far more than any substantial common program.

Contemporary constructive religious thought has manifested such a range of specific interests that it is difficult to offer summary comments about it as a field. Perhaps the one characteristic shared widely is the essential modesty and personal reference in terms of which this literature is written. For example, the most influential recent contemporary Roman Catholic statement is Hans Küng's *On Being a Christian* (1976). Placed beside traditional statements, it is tentative and searching and, in comparison with traditional Roman Catholic dogmatic theology, the Church as an institution is greatly deemphasized. David Tracy, in his *Blessed Rage for Order* (1975), suggests directions being taken by younger American Roman Catholic theologians. Themes of reflection within Jewish circles have moved out from the unimaginable horror of the Holocaust as a point of departure, since by the end of World War II the great European Jewish community had been virtually destroyed. Some of this reflection is taken up in more specifically literary forms, as in the widely admired writings of Elie Wiesel. Others, like Richard Rubenstein, have been more concerned with the issue of the Holocaust as the basis for systematic reflection about human life.

Among Protestants, the dominant theme has been liberation, but the significant query is, liberation from what? For black Americans, racial oppression has been the dominant theme. For those critical of capitalism and its inequalities, a broad reconciliation of Marxist perspectives with Christian convictions has been the overriding issue. For those impressed with the stultifying effects of affluence, psychological liberation has been a recurring subject. Thus the theme of liberation represents even less coherence and deep generational identity for current theologians than neo-orthodoxy represented for those grouped under that heading thirty or more years ago. If any single figure might be said to have mediated between the great generation, represented by figures like Barth on the continent and the Niebuhr brothers on this side of the Atlantic, and the successor generation, it would be Dietrich Bonhoeffer, himself a man of both worlds. As a young scholar in the 1930s, Bonhoeffer had studied at Union Theological Seminary in New York. Having returned to his homeland, he lost his life in the struggle against Hitler. But through his writings his influence returned across the Atlantic to make him a major voice in the post neo-orthodox phase of constructive religious thought. But Bonhoeffer's writings do not present a finished system so much as a bridge to newer concerns about the secular world that has been the hallmark of the last decades.

Certainly among American scholars the most consistent critical attention to the problem of constructive religious thought in modern culture has been given by Van A. Harvey. In *The Historian and the Believer: The Morality of Historical Knowledge and Christian Belief* (1966) he explicitly analyzed the intellectual sources of the current cultural situation. Subsequently, Harvey has been interested in the status of the alienated theologian. In this he describes exactly the position of the religious thinker whose counterpart in an earlier era had a relatively secure relationship with a traditional body of faith and a location in a supportive community, however he might stand in a critical relationship to it. Such a position made it possible for him to develop individual and collective self-understandings that were more generally plausible. In some sense the new factor Harvey has recognized is not only the pluralism of religious institutions and traditions, but the very conceptualization of religion as a species of cultural activity.

Another significant approach to this question of the changing forms of religious thought is represented in the work of Hans Frei, who might best be described as a cultural historian. Depending very much on the literary perspectives developed by Erich Auerbach, Frei has charted the deep shift in theology between Medieval and modern cultures. In the phrase that gives title to his major work, there has been an "eclipse of biblical narrative"; in other words, the tradition of figural interpretation of scripture gave way under the pressure of the critical impulses of the Enlightenment. Whereas constructive theological work had, in earlier eras, been premised upon the scriptures as in some sense providing the pattern on which the world was created and recreated, under the corrosive influence of the Enlightenment the biblical books became simply a particular literature. The work of Frei and Harvey indicates how the conceptualization of religion, which took its general rise from the Enlightenment, has profoundly shifted the ground upon which constructive religious thinking goes on in contemporary culture.

Barth, Karl. *Against the Stream: Shorter Post-War Writings, 1946–1952.* Ed. by R. G. Smith. London: SCM Press, 1954.
————. *Church Dogmatics.* Ed. by G. W. Bromily and T. F. Torrance. Edinburgh: T. and T. Clark, 1936–69. 4v. in 12.
————. *Dogmatics in Outline.* London: SCM Press, 1949.
Bonhoeffer, Dietrich. *The Cost of Discipleship.* Tr. by R. H. Fuller. New York: Macmillan, 1959.
————. *Letters and Papers from Prison.* Ed. by E. Bethge. London: SCM Press, 1967.
Bultmann, Rudolf. *Existence and Faith: Shorter Writings of Rudolf Bultmann.* Ed. by Schubert Ogden. New York: Meridian Books, 1960.
————. *Jesus Christ and Mythology.* New York: Scribner's, 1958.
————. *The Presence of Eternity: History and Eschatology.* Edinburgh: Edinburgh Univ. Pr., 1957.
Cone, James H. *A Black Theology of Liberation.* Philadelphia: Lippincott, 1970.
————. *God of the Oppressed.* New York: Seabury, 1975.
Cox, Harvey. *The Secular City.* New York: Macmillan, 1965.
Frei, Hans. *The Eclipse of Biblical Narrative: A Study in 18th and 19th Century Hermeneutics.* New Haven, Conn.: Yale Univ. Pr., 1974.
————. *The Identity of Jesus Christ: The Hermeneutical Basis of Dogmatic Theology.* Philadelphia: Fortress, 1975.
Gilkey, Langdon. *Naming the Whirlwind: The Renewal of God-language.* Indianapolis, Ind.: Bobbs-Merrill, 1969.

————. *Reaping the Whirlwind: A Christian Interpretation of History.* New York: Seabury, 1976.

Gilson, Etienne. *History of Christian Philosophy in the Middle Ages.* New York: Random House, 1955.

Harvey, Van A. *The Historian and the Believer: The Morality of Historical Knowledge and Christian Belief.* New York: Macmillan, 1966.

Heschel, Abraham. *God in Search of Man: A Philosophy of Judaism.* New York: Farrar, Straus & Cudahy, 1955.

————. *Man's Quest for God: Studies in Prayer and Symbolism.* New York: Scribner's, 1954.

Küng, Hans. *Freedom Today.* New York: Sheed & Ward, 1966.

————. *On Being a Christian.* Garden City, N.Y.: Doubleday, 1976.

Maritain, Jacques. *Man and the State.* Chicago: Univ. of Chicago Pr., 1951.

————. *Scholasticism and Politics.* New York: Macmillan, 1940.

Moltmann, Jurgen. *Theology of Hope.* New York: Harper & Row, 1967.

Niebuhr, H. Richard. *Christ and Culture.* New York: Harper & Row, 1951.

————. *Radical Monotheism and Western Culture.* New York: Harper & Row, 1960.

Niebuhr, Reinhold. *Moral Man and Immoral Society.* New York: Scribner's, 1932.

————. *The Nature and Destiny of Man.* New York: Scribner's, 1941, 1943. 2v.

————. *The Self and the Dramas of History.* New York: Scribner's, 1955.

Ogden, Schubert. *Christ Without Myth.* New York: Harper & Row, 1961.

————. *The Reality of God and Other Essays.* New York: Harper & Row, 1966.

Rubenstein, Richard. *After Auschwitz: Radical Theology and Contemporary Judaism.* Indianapolis, Ind.: Bobbs-Merrill, 1966.

————. *My Brother Paul.* New York: Harper & Row, 1972.

Schaull, M. Richard. *Encounter with Revolution.* New York: Association Pr., 1955.

Tillich, Paul. *Dynamics of Faith.* New York: Harper & Row, 1957.

————. *Systematic Theology.* Chicago: Univ. of Chicago Pr., 1967. 3v. in 1.

Tracy, David. *Blessed Rage for Order: The New Pluralism in Theology.* New York: Seabury, 1975.

Vahanian, Gabriel. *The Death of God: The Culture of Our Post-Christian Era.* New York: Braziller, 1961.

Van Buren, Paul. *The Secular Meaning of the Gospel.* New York: Macmillan, 1963.

Wiesel, Elie. *Messengers of God: Biblical Portraits and Legends.* New York: Random House, 1976.

————. *Souls on Fire: Portraits and Legends of Hasidic Masters.* New York: Random House, 1972.

RELIGIOUS ETHICS

For the reasons just suggested regarding contemporary religious thought, the issue of the religious norms governing behavior has also become a critical scholarly issue in the course of recent decades. The uncertain social reality of traditional religious communities, and the confusion engendered by location in religiously plural cultures, has been reflected in a marked diffusion of constructive religious thought. These same factors have worked to an opposite effect with respect to religious ethics. The question of what behavior is appropriate to religiously sensitive people has been intensified by cultural conditions. The comparatively sharp focus of discussions about religious ethics was signaled by the founding of a Society for Religious Ethics within the last decade, which has sponsored a new and successful *Journal of Religious Ethics* (1973–). In addition, interaction with philosophical ethicists and others concerned with professional ethics has led to ongoing discussions. The comparative vitality of religious ethics, then, derives from the reality of a religiously plural, not to say compound, society, much as the diversity and differences of religious thought reflect, albeit in opposite ways, the same social conditions. The different religious traditions and modes of reflection simply yield various perspectives on concrete social issues in common life. Of course a reciprocal effect is also involved—a pushing back against religious traditions and communities out of the complex social world.

Among concrete issues, none has led to wider ethical reflection than questions about determination of ethical norms in relationship to medical procedures. The sources of this development are obvious. Striking advances in medical practices and the availability of public funds to support continued research as well as to fund health care on an increasingly broad basis has led to enormously complex issues about very basic traditional questions. For example, the definition of "death" (and that of "life," for that matter) among humans has been rendered exceedingly complex by procedures that enable medical teams to keep the body "alive" when virtually all brain activity has ceased. At what point do ethical considerations cease to call for continued support for life? And how do discriminations based upon conditions that have obtained across millennia come to terms with new circumstances that have been literally unimaginable up to this point? Or how does the ancient prohibition against euthanasia appear in the context of current life-sustaining medical practices? The same kind of enormously complex ethical and moral issues that surround death are raised at the other end as well, with respect to the beginning of life. Clearly human life is well under way before the mother's experience of "quickening"—which represented the conventional beginning point of life for much of Western morality. Thanks to modern medicine we now recognize that at such a point the fetus is already securely developed and rapidly becoming a recognizable and viable human life. Does this drive the religiously sensitive person, especially within the Roman Catholic moral tradition, back toward the moment of conception as the logical beginning point for life? The ethical implications of these questions are many and basic. It is in no way surprising that the review of these issues has engaged medical practitioners along with moral and religious philosophers in continuing and searching exchanges.

In a similar way, religious ethicists have been drawn into review of and reflection upon the nature of modern war and its limits. Here again, the issue has not been absent from religiously sponsored moral and ethical reflection in the Western tradition. Given the refinement in the techniques of war making and the compression of time and extension of power involved in the modern world, however, there have been corresponding ramifications of the issues of war into political life generally. It is not difficult, therefore, to explain reasons for the development of a ready interest in these questions among religiously sensitive ethicists.

The other element in the contemporary development of religious ethics has been a systematic reflection back upon traditional sources of religious morality. The experience of new and pressing social issues has resulted in the attempt to reassess the traditions and reappropriate them. Examples of this more systematic concern are provided in Gene H. Outka, *Agape: An Ethical Analysis* (1972) and James M. Gustafson, *Theology and Christian Ethics* (1974). At the same time there have been major attempts to restate the ethical dimensions of religious traditions among European religious communities. Helmut Thielicke represents the Lutheran tradition in this respect. This recovery of an interest in ethical perspectives within religious communities has also been influenced by a return to more strictly ethical concerns among philosophers per se; for example, in the writings of John Rawls.

Several additional dimensions of this issue require attention. First is a recent impulse toward comparative study of religious ethics. In the consciousness of religious pluralism in American society, the range of ethical positions internal to Western religious life is obvious. But recognizing other cultures and their religiously authorized patterns of behavior point to a still further variety of ethical positions. There is an interesting parallel with recent religious thought at this point; Paul Tillich and Thomas Merton both discovered Buddhism and cultivated their interest in it at the ends of their careers. Most recently this question has also been explored by Harvey Cox.

An additional dimension concerns reflection back upon the sources for ethics in the theoretical literature of the social sciences. More than in the case of religious thought, ethical reflection has focused on both the social locations of behavior under religious norms and the data increasingly available through the social sciences regarding this problematic. This situation has entailed, on the one hand, renewed interest in such figures as Max Weber and Ernst Troeltsch, as well as continued interest in the reflective knowledge produced by social scientists about human communities in which ethical actors are located.

In conclusion, it is important to reemphasize the difference between the course of development with respect to ethical reflection and that of recent developments in religious thought. In one sense this is because religious thought has tended to become severed from communities of religious belief and behavior. But it is also because constructive religious ethical reflection must necessarily come to terms with concrete and difficult policy issues. In some sense, constructive religious thinkers have had the luxury of floating free, so to speak, from the realities of human behavior. As a consequence, their writings have not been rooted in communities and traditions that, historically at least, have nourished constructive religious thought.

Childress, James. *Civil Disobedience and Political Obligation: A Study in Christian Social Ethics*. New Haven, Conn.: Yale Univ. Pr., 1971.

Green, Ronald. *Religious Reason*. New York: Oxford Univ. Pr., 1978.

Gustafson, James M. *Christ and the Moral Life*. New York: Harper & Row, 1968.

———. *Theology and Christian Ethics*. Philadelphia: United Church Pr., 1974.

Johnson, James T. *Ideology, Reason and the Limitation of War: Religious and Secular Concepts, 1200–1740*. Princeton, N.J.: Princeton Univ. Pr., 1975.

Little, David, and Sumner Twiss. *Comparative Religious Ethics*. New York: Harper & Row, 1978.

Noonan, John T. *Contraception: A History of Its Treatment by the Catholic Theologians and Canonists*. Cambridge, Mass.: Belknap Pr. of Harvard Univ. Pr., 1965.

Outka, Gene H. *Agape: An Ethical Analysis*. New Haven, Conn.: Yale Univ. Pr., 1972.

———, and John P. Reeder. *Religion and Morality: A Collection of Essays*. Garden City, N.Y.: Doubleday, 1973.

Ramsey, Paul. *Deeds and Rules in Christian Ethics*. New York: Scribner's, 1967.

———. *The Patient as Person: Explorations in Medical Ethics*. New Haven, Conn.: Yale Univ. Pr., 1970.

Rawls, John. *A Theory of Justice*. Cambridge, Mass.: Belknap Pr. of Harvard Univ. Pr., 1971.

Thielicke, Helmut. *Theological Ethics*. Ed. by W. H. Lazareth. Philadelphia: Fortress, 1966–69. 2v.

5

The Scientific Study
of Religion

In the introductory sections of this essay, references were made to the legacies of Max Weber and Emile Durkheim. Their larger enterprises have continued to inform scholarly traditions of anthropology and sociology and to make the question of religion as a social given productive. At the same time, this tradition of social thought also stands behind a more technical subfield, the sociology of religion. In the last several decades there has been rather important development of it along certain lines. In the 1930s and 1940s, the work of Weber and his contemporary, Ernst Troeltsch, continued to influence religious scholarship through the writings of the Niebuhr brothers, especially Richard Niebuhr's *Social Sources of Denominationalism* (1929) and the general preoccupations of Reinhold Niebuhr. But in the subsequent decades there has been a more specific indebtedness to this tradition of social thought.

On the theoretical side, an attempt has been made to refine Weberian categories of analysis as applied to religion. One example of this is Paul M. Harrison's *Authority and Power in the Free Church Tradition: A Social Case Study of the American Baptist Convention* (1959), an analysis of bureaucratic behavior in churches committed to voluntary principles of organization. Another is David Little's *Religion, Order and Law: A Study in Pre-Revolutionary England* (1969).

In a more general sense, Peter L. Berger has been at the center of this field for two decades. In his understanding of religion and its relationship to culture especially in the modern world, he is deeply influenced by Max Weber. In collaboration with Thomas Luckmann he has concentrated upon sociology of knowledge: *The Social Construction of Reality* (1966). It represents a significant theoretical development that has been widely influential beyond the narrow field of sociology of religion. Subsequently he has moved on to be concerned with secularization in his book *The Sacred Canopy* (1967). In this connection, see Luckmann's more radical statement with respect to religion in modern society: *The Invisible Religion* (1967). Max Weber's shadow has also been cast across a variety of other sociological studies such as Gerhard Lenski's *The Religious Factor* (1961).

A recent figure standing in this tradition, with more explicit indebtedness to Emile Durkheim, is Robert Bellah. His initial major study was entitled *Tokugawa Religion* (cited on page 41). In some respects this was a parallel to Max Weber's highly influential *The Protestant Ethic and the Spirit of Capitalism* (cited on page 15). See also *Religion and Progress in Modern Asia,* which Bellah edited (1965). More recently, Bellah has stimulated discussion of civil religion, first in lectures and essays and then through a book titled *The Broken Covenant* (1975). In general he is concerned to explore the collective religious prerequisites of American life. The civil religion exchanges are most readily available in a single volume edited by Russell Richey and Donald Jones called *American Civil Religion* (1974). See also John F. Wilson's *Public Religion in American Culture* (1979). A collection of separate pieces by Bellah suggests how his interests in strictly sociological issues merge with impulses to engage in more constructive religious thought: *Beyond Belief: Essays on Religion in a Post-traditional World* (1970).

Current directions in sociology of religion are probably best seen in several recent books by a younger scholar, Robert Wuthnow: *The Consciousness Reformation* (1976) and *Experimentation in American Religion* (1978). On the one hand, he undertakes to analyze data from survey research in a highly sophisticated manner. On the other, his studies show sensitivity to the theoretical side of the field that continues to be deeply indebted to Weber. For general introductions to the field, several studies are useful, among them Michael Hill, *The Sociology of Religion* (1973) and Roland Robertson, *The Sociological Interpretation of Religion* (1973).

There is general agreement both that the field of psychology of religion holds a great deal of promise, and that at the same time it has not fostered the scholarship of which it is capable. As Max Weber and Emile Durkheim cast shadows over current discussions in sociology of religion, Sigmund Freud, Carl Jung, and William James are still influential in this field. In this case, however, scholarly discussions have been far less sharply focused. Erik Erikson's concern with ego psychology seemed to be one especially promising development. Interest in the phenomenon of conversion has also been marked. But in the psychology of religion there has not been the concerted application of theoretical resources to scholarly projects that has made the sociology of religion a highly productive field.

Scholarly discussion in sociology and psychology of religion is facilitated by an active professional organization, The Society for the Scientific Study of Religion, which meets annually. It sponsors a scholarly journal, the *Journal for the Scientific Study of Religion,* in which current interests can be gauged. A set of essays that reflects these interests and addresses the issue of new directions in the scientific study of religion is Charles Y. Glock and Phillip E. Hammond (editors), *Beyond the Classics? Essays in the Scientific Study of Religion* (1973).

Bellah, Robert. *Beyond Belief: Essays on Religion in a Post-traditional World.* New York: Harper & Row, 1970.

————. *The Broken Covenant.* New York: Seabury, 1975.

————, ed. *Religion and Progress in Modern Asia.* New York: Free Pr., 1965.

Berger, Peter L. *The Sacred Canopy.* Garden City, N.Y.: Doubleday, 1967.

————, and Thomas Luckmann. *The Social Construction of Reality.* Garden City, N.Y.: Doubleday, 1966.

Erikson, Erik H. *Young Man Luther.* New York: Norton, 1958.

Freud, Sigmund. *Civilization and Its Discontents.* London: Hogarth, 1957.

————. *The Future of an Illusion.* New York: Liveright, 1953.

————. *Totem and Taboo.* London: Routledge, 1919.

Glock, Charles Y., and Phillip E. Hammond. *Beyond the Classics? Essays in the Scientific Study of Religion.* New York: Harper & Row, 1973.

Harrison, Paul M. *Authority and Power in the Free Church Tradition: A Social Case Study of the American Baptist Convention.* Princeton, N.J.: Princeton Univ. Pr., 1959.

Hill, Michael. *The Sociology of Religion.* New York: Basic Books, 1973.

James, William. *The Varieties of Religious Experience.* New York: Modern Library, 1902.

Jung, Carl G. *The Archetypes and the Collective Unconscious, Collected Works IX/1.* New York: Pantheon, 1959.

————. *Psychology and Religion: West and East, Collected Works II.* New York: Pantheon, 1958.

Lenski, Gerhard. *The Religious Factor.* Garden City, N.Y.: Doubleday, 1961.

Little, David. *Religion, Order and Law: A Study in Pre-Revolutionary England.* New York: Harper, 1969.

Luckmann, Thomas. *The Invisible Religion.* New York: Macmillan, 1967.

Niebuhr, H. Richard. *The Social Sources of Denominationalism.* New York: Holt, 1929.

Richey, Russell, and Donald Jones. *American Civil Religion.* New York: Harper & Row, 1974.

Robertson, Roland. *The Sociological Interpretation of Religion.* New York: Schocken Books, 1973.

Wilson, John F. *Public Religion in American Culture.* Philadelphia: Temple Univ. Pr., 1979.

Wuthnow, Robert. *The Consciousness Reformation.* Berkeley: Univ. of California Pr., 1976.

————. *Experimentation in American Religion.* Berkeley: Univ. of California Pr., 1978.

PART II

REFERENCE WORKS

General Works

ATLASES

Al Faruqi, Isma'il Ragi, ed.; David E. Sopher, map ed. *Historical Atlas of the Religions of the World.* New York: Macmillan, 1974. 346p.

This atlas is composed of several scholarly essays on the histories of the world's religions, integrated with maps, tables, charts, and photographs of artistic creations, all designed to show the relationships between people and their religions to the surrounding cultural and geographic environments. The material is divided first into sections for religions of the past, ethnic religions of the present, and universal religions of the present, and then into specific areas and religions. Appended are basic chronologies for religions of the past and of the present with the latter containing subdivisions for particular faiths. Indexes of subjects and of proper names are included.

Gaustad, Edwin Scott. *Historical Atlas of Religion in America.* Rev. ed. New York: Harper & Row, 1976. 189p.

Gaustad, while recognizing the difficulties involved in defining such terms as church and membership and in drawing statistical comparisons of them, has attempted to describe and analyze the paths of religion in America. He concentrates on Christianity since 1650 but also deals with other groups. He believes the major characteristics of American religious thought and institutions to be individualism, experimentalism, atavism, nativism, probabalism, and denominationalism. The maps, text, charts, and tables are integrated and deal primarily with the locations of churches and ecclesiastical boundaries and with membership growth curves. Appendixes contain additional statistical information. The indexes deal separately with authors and titles, places, religious bodies, and names and subjects.

BIBLIOGRAPHY

Adams, Charles Joseph, ed. *A Reader's Guide to the Great Religions.* 2d ed. New York: Free Pr., 1977. 521p.

This work is a collection of thirteen signed articles on the primary religious divisions of mankind. Each article, written by an expert in the field, is a narrative discussion of the basic elements of the faith with an emphasis on primary and secondary sources. Regional and biographical sections are included in the articles, as well as sections on religious concepts and historical

107

events. There are an author and subject index and an appendix, "The History of the History of Religion."

Barrow, John G. *A Bibliography of Bibliographies in Religion.* Ann Arbor, Mich.: Edwards Bros., 1955. 489p.

This bibliography, started as a 1929 Yale doctoral dissertation, is divided into several topical areas such as church history, non-Christian religions, the Reformation, sects, sermons, and individuals. Most of these topics are further subdivided either topically or geographically. Under these headings, the titles are listed in chronological order according to the date of publication. For each bibliography cited, the author provides the full title, publishing information, size, pagination, and a location key as well as an evaluative note in many cases. The bibliography is wide-ranging but does omit certain categories of bibliographies, such as those appended to books and articles, lists of incunabula, indexes of prohibited books, and some dealers' catalogs. The preface provides a full listing of the omissions. An appendix lists bibliographies brought to Barrow's attention but which he could neither examine nor about which could he find any indication of quality. A list of references and an index to proper names conclude the volume.

Berkowitz, Morris I., and J. Edmund Johnson. *Social Scientific Studies of Religion: A Bibliography.* n.p.: Univ. of Pittsburgh Pr., 1967. 258p.

This bibliography contains over 6,000 unannotated citations to journal articles and books published or reprinted since 1945. Only publications appearing in English are included. The compilers view religion as a universal phenomenon and as a key cultural element, and they have stressed an interdisciplinary approach. The citations are listed under nine major subject and form headings and subdivisions thereof, such as history and development of religion, religion and social issues, the impact of religious belief on behavior, and religion and social change. Cross-references are noted at the ends of sections. The work concludes with an index of journals consulted, abbreviations used, and an author index.

Boyd, George N., and Lois A. Boyd. *Religion in Contemporary Fiction: Criticism from 1945 to the Present.* San Antonio, Tex.: Trinity Univ. Pr., 1973. 99p.

The Boyds's work cites books and journal articles in English written since 1945 and pertaining primarily to English-language novelists. The first half of the book cites publications under headings for theological motifs and themes, such as grace, reconciliation, and the Apocalypse; under selected topics, such as black fiction, morality, and violence; and under selected authors, such as Salinger, Malamud, and Barth. The second major section lists works on religion and aesthetics, the arts, literary criticism, and literary imagination. Each item is numbered, and cross-references are noted whenever appropriate. The final section is a list of other relevant bibliographies. Primary and secondary author indexes are included.

Burr, Nelson R. *A Critical Bibliography of Religion in America.* Princeton, N.J.: Princeton Univ. Pr., 1961. 2v. (Religion in American Life ser.)

Burr has written bibliographical essays to conclude the series *Religion in American Life*. The five major parts deal with bibliographic guides, the evolution of American religion, religion and society, religion in the arts and literature, and intellectual history, theology, philosophy, and science. Each part contains several topical subdivisions. Burr did not aim at comprehensiveness but rather sought to include important, representative works. Books, articles, theses, and pamphlets are among the many diversified works examined. An author index is included.

Capps, Donald; Lewis Rambo; and Paul Ransohoff. *Psychology of Religion: A Guide to Information Sources.* Detroit: Gale, 1976. 352p. (Philosophy and Religion Information Guide ser., v.1)
This work is a bibliography of the psychology of religion divided into sections on general works, the mythological dimension of religion, the ritual dimension, the experiential dimension, the dispositional dimension, the social dimension, and the directional dimension. There are separate author, title, and subject indexes. The entries include books and journal articles and are selectively annotated. The period covered is from 1950–74 with emphasis on 1960–74 in light of the fact that the earlier years are covered in W. W. Meissner's *Annotated Bibliography in Religion and Psychology* (New York: Academy of Religion and Mental Health, 1961. 235p.).

International Bibliography of the History of Religions. Leiden: Brill, 1952– .
This work includes material on all areas and religions. It lists both books and periodical articles.

Mitros, Joseph F. *Religions: A Select, Classified Bibliography.* New York: Learned, 1973. 435p.
This book is a guide for students of religion. The first part of the work deals with research in this discipline; the major section of the book, however, is a list of materials of many eras and places. Included are original and secondary sources, with special attention given to reference works and scholarly periodicals. Most of the materials are in English, although a few foreign-language titles are included. Brief annotations are provided for some of the entries, and an index of names is appended.

Morris, Raymond P. *A Theological Book List.* n.p.: Theological Education Fund, 1960. 242p., 41p., 49p., 30p., 21p.
————. ————. Supplement. 1963. 43p.
These lists were compiled to assist in improving theological libraries in Africa, Asia, and Latin America. The original volume contains primarily books in English, whereas the supplement is divided into sections for English, French, German, Portuguese, and Spanish publications. The citations are unannotated and are arranged under such subject areas as Bible, Hellenistic Judaism, theology, patristic period, worship, and ethics. Some works on non-Christian religions are included. The original volume has an author index, as do each of the language supplements.

Regazzi, John J., and Theodore C. Hines. *A Guide to Indexed Periodicals in Religion.* Metuchen, N.J.: Scarecrow, 1975. 314p.

This work was partially conceived as a supplement to other serial guides and as an index to them. It contains four principal sections which, taken as a whole, provide in one place a great deal of information that was previously scattered. The sections are: (1) a list of the indexing and abstracting services, together with their mnemonic abbreviations, that are covered; (2) an alphabetical list of the periodicals covered, followed by the service abbreviation(s); (3) an inverted entry list by key title words similar to number 2; and (4) lists, by service, of the periodicals each one covers.

BIOGRAPHY

Bowden, Henry Warner. *Dictionary of American Religious Biography.* Westport, Conn.: Greenwood, 1977. 572p.

This volume contains biographies of 425 American religious figures who died before 1 July 1976. The persons chosen for entry represent a wide range of denominations, backgrounds, and approaches. Increase Mather, Abraham Joshua Heschel, Martin Luther King, and Eusebio Francisco Kino, among many others, are included. Each biography begins with personal, educational, and career data, proceeds with a narrative sketch, and ends with a select bibliography of works by and about the subject. Appended are listings of the individuals by denomination and birthplace. A subject index is also included.

DICTIONARIES AND ENCYCLOPEDIAS

Avi-Yonah, Michael. *Encyclopedia of Archaeological Excavations in the Holy Land.* Englewood Cliffs, N.J.: Prentice-Hall, 1975. 4v.

Originally published in Hebrew in two volumes, this work was compiled in cooperation with the Israel Exploration Society of Jerusalem. Alphabetic entries cover each excavation site. Composite articles on churches, monasteries, synagogues, and specific geographic areas are also included. The time span is from prehistoric times through the Crusades. Illustrations in black and white and in color, many of which were prepared especially for this work, supplement the text. Chronological tables, maps, and plans are also included. The last volume includes a glossary of Hebrew terms and indexes to names and places.

Brandon, S. G. F., ed. *Dictionary of Comparative Religion.* New York: Scribner's, 1970. 704p.

This work deals with the major and minor faiths from Buddhism and Islam to the Carthaginian and Harranian religions. The former are covered by way of several entries of varying lengths dealing with such aspects as doctrine, sects, symbols, and important persons. The latter are covered in single comprehensive articles. All of the entries are initialed, with a key at the front of the volume. Most include bibliographies and cross-references. The length of the articles ranges from a paragraph to several pages. Added features include a brief essay on the pronunciation of words in non-European languages, a general index, and a synoptic index for the major religions. The synoptic index provides a unifying framework by listing under the name of a religion, such as Judaism, or the name of a country, such as Japan, all of those related terms to be found in the dictionary.

Hastings, James, et al., eds. *Encyclopedia of Religion and Ethics.* New York: Scribner's, 1908–27. 12v. and index v.

This work contains articles on all religions and all the great ethical systems. It has articles on beliefs, customs, ethical movements, philosophical ideas, and moral practices. It is strong on biography. It embraces theology, philosophy, anthropology, mythology, folklore, biology, psychology, economics, and sociology. It has both general and specific articles. The contributors represent the finest liberal Protestant scholarship available at the time of publication.

Jackson, Samuel Macauley, et al., eds. *The New Schaff-Herzog Encyclopedia of Religious Knowledge.* Based on the 3d ed. of the *Realencyklopädie* founded by J. J. Herzog and ed. by Albert Hauck. New York: Funk & Wagnalls, 1908–21. 12v. and index. Repr.: Grand Rapids, Mich.: Baker Book House, 1949–50. 12v.; index, v.13, 1954.

This work was prepared by more than 600 scholars and specialists. Philip Schaff adapted the encyclopedia to the American public. It contains hundreds of biographies, the material for which was provided by the subjects in many cases. It is rich in bibliography. The set is supplemented by *Twentieth Century Encyclopedia of Religious Knowledge,* edited by Lefferts A. Loetscher et al. (Grand Rapids, Mich.: Baker Book House, 1955).

Kauffman, Donald T. *The Dictionary of Religious Terms.* Westwood, N.J.: Revell, 1967.

This dictionary contains several thousand concise, objective definitions of key religious terms and terms related to religion from all faiths, regardless of their size or importance, through the ages. While the definitions are brief, they attempt to place the work in some context. Many entries are biographical, although living persons are not included unless they are integrally related to larger contemporary issues or events. For words with additional meanings outside the religious context, only the religious definition is noted. Terms within an entry for which a separate notation has been written are indicated by small capitals. One small shortcoming of the work is the lack of a key indicating the standard transliteration used from non-Roman alphabets.

Loetscher, Lefferts A., et al., eds. *Twentieth Century Encyclopedia of Religious Knowledge.* Grand Rapids, Mich.: Baker Book House, 1955.

This work supplements the *New Schaff-Herzog Encyclopedia of Religious Knowledge* (repr.: Grand Rapids, Mich.: Baker Book House, 1949–50. 13v.). Social and cultural changes, the discovery of new source materials, new presuppositions and techniques, as well as new events, institutions, and personalities led to its development. Like the main set, this work provides data on both Christian and non-Christian religions.

Parrinder, Geoffrey. *A Dictionary of Non-Christian Religions.* Philadelphia: Westminster Pr., 1971. 320p.

Parrinder's work deals with the beliefs, practices, and deities of the non-Christian religions except those mentioned in the Bible, because Christianity and biblical subjects are dealt with at length in other reference sources. Special attention is given to Hinduism, Buddhism, and Islam as the three largest non-Christian faiths; but the classical world, post-biblical Judaism, the Americas, Australasia, and Africa receive substantial attention. Entries deal with religion and religion-related subjects as well as with philosophical schools. Cross-references guide the reader to related subjects. The text is enriched with many photographs and drawings and is appended by lists of dynasties from Egypt, the Islamic Empire, and China as well as by a list for further reading.

Zaehner, R. C., ed. *The Concise Encyclopedia of Living Faiths.* Boston: Beacon Pr., 1967. 431p.

This work deals with Judaism, Christianity, Islam, Zoroastrianism, Hinduism, Jainism, Buddhism, Shintoism, Confucianism, and Taoism. The stress is on Christianity and Buddhism. Each chapter is treated historically. The book is designed for the general reader.

DIRECTORIES

Geisendorfer, James V., ed. cons. *Directory of Religious Organizations in the United States of America.* Washington, N.C.: McGrath, 1977. 553p. (A Consortium Book)

This work is a classified listing of 1,569 religious and secular organizations in the field of religion including national departments of churches, professional associations, volunteer groups, religious orders, government agencies, businesses, foundations, and fraternal societies. Arranged in nine sections according to their major purposes, large and small organizations of many denominations in the United States are noted. With information supplied by the organizations, each entry gives religious affiliation, address, telephone number, name of the chief executive officer and membership figures. An Index of Organizational Titles affords further access.

Melton, J. Gordon, and James V. Geisendorfer. *A Directory of Religious Bodies in the United States.* New York: Garland, 1977. 225p.

Nearly 1,300 religious groups, including some not found in the *Handbook of Denominations,* are listed in this work. The arrangement is alphabetical, and the address of each body is provided along with titles of its publications. In the second part of the volume, Melton attempts to develop a classified arrangement of religious bodies. Denominations and sects are listed under a number of broad groupings, such as the "Baptist Family," the "Lutheran Family," "Non-Christian Groups," and even such unusual ones as "Neo-Paganism" and "Mail Order Churches." In this section the founding date of each group is given. A selective bibliography of materials relating to American religious bodies completes the volume.

GUIDES AND HANDBOOKS

Carroll, Jackson W.; Douglas W. Johnson; and Martin E. Marty. *Religion in America, 1950 to the Present.* New York: Harper & Row, 1979. 123p.

Part I, a sociological diagnosis of American religion, includes statistics on religious membership, church attendance, practices, and beliefs. In Part II, American religious pluralism is described and analyzed through the use of maps to show the distribution of denominations. In Part III, predictions on the future of religion in America are offered. In the final prognosis, George Gallup predicts a religious revival; this section is accompanied by statistics on religious practices and beliefs.

Kennedy, James R. *Library Research Guide to Religion and Theology: Illustrated Search Strategy and Sources.* Ann Arbor, Mich.: Pierian Pr., 1974. 53p. (Library Research Guides ser., no. 1)

This book is designed for the advanced undergraduate religion major and graduate students in the field. The work assumes no previous background and contains a "Library Knowledge Test" as a useful appendix for initial evaluation. The first chapters deal with choosing and narrowing topics and are followed by chapters devoted to the card catalog, evaluating sources, finding quotations, and using other guides and sources. A concise bibliography for religious studies is appended. Illustrated.

Landis, Benson Y. *World Religions: A Brief Guide to the Principal Beliefs and Teachings of the Religions of the World and to the Statistics of Organized Religion.* Rev. ed. New York: Dutton, 1965. 127p.

Landis's book, designed for the layperson interested in a general and descriptive, rather than scholarly or technical, overview of religion, describes forty major religions of the world, giving concise information on beliefs and teachings of different religious groups, their history, statistics, and recent developments. The book emphasizes the religions of the United States, Canada, and Great Britain. The religions are arranged alphabetically, with cross-references. A glossary and an index complete the work.

Rosten, Leo, ed. *Religions of America: Ferment and Faith in an Age of Crisis: A New Guide and Almanac.* New York: Simon & Schuster, 1975. 672p.

Rosten's survey of American religions is composed of two main parts. The first consists of nineteen essays on specific faiths and on agnostics, unaffiliated religious persons, and scientists. The author of each essay has responded to questions on the group's beliefs, attitudes on current issues, and history as a separate group. The second section is an almanac that contains miscellaneous facts, surveys, and court decisions about and affecting religion and religious issues, both doctrinal and social. Statistics and censuses are also included. Rosten has frequently added interpretation and commentary. A glossary and an index are included.

INDEXES AND ABSTRACT JOURNALS

American Theological Library Association. *Religion Index One: Periodicals, 1949/1952–*. Chicago: American Theological Library Assn., 1953– .
Until 1975 this index was published in two parts. The first cited articles under author and subject headings, and the second cited book reviews. Beginning in 1975, the compilation of the index has been produced through the use of the computer, and the listings appear in three sections. The first is a subject index, the second an author index with abstracts provided for many of the articles by the authors, and the third is a book review index. Although preference is given to articles written in English, the index remains international in scope. Before July, 1977, this work was entitled *Index to Religious Periodical Literature*.

QUOTATIONS

Mead, Frank S., ed. and comp. *The Encyclopedia of Religious Quotations*. Westwood, N.J.: Revell, 1965. 534p.
Arranged in topical order, the quotations included cover the gamut of particular religions and religion in general. Some of the subject headings employed are covetousness, God, immortality, time, mother, and work. When possible, the editor identified the author of the quote, gave her or his dates, and noted the work in which the quotation appeared. At the end is an author index and a detailed index of topics.

Woods, Ralph L. *The World Treasury of Religious Quotations*. New York: Hawthorn Books, 1966. 1,106p.
This volume lists several thousand quotations dealing with religious subjects as well as general topics, such as labor unions and nuclear energy, approached from a religious point of view. The work is nondenominational, and a wide range of views appears, including those of authors as diverse as Martin Luther, Karl Marx, Norman Vincent Peale, and Wernher Von Braun. Quotations from the Bible and biblical commentaries are excluded. The arrangement is alphabetical by subject and has cross-references as well as an author index.

Mysticism

Ferguson, John. *An Illustrated Encyclopedia of Mysticism and the Mystery Religions*. London: Thames & Hudson, 1976. 228p.
Ferguson has provided concise, alphabetically arranged sketches and explanations of mystics and terms relating to mysticism from around the world and throughout the ages. One finds, for example, entries for kabbalah, Teresa de Jesus, pentecostalism, Bodhidharma, and Vedanta Hinduism. Ferguson has, however, avoided the areas of demonology, magic, and witchcraft. Cross-references are plentiful, and many illustrations enrich the text. A bibliography is appended.

DICTIONARIES AND ENCYCLOPEDIAS

Evans, Bergen. *Dictionary of Mythology, Mainly Classical.* Lincoln, Nebr.: Centennial Pr., 1970. 293p.

This volume is an alphabetically arranged encyclopedia with entries for mythological characters, concepts, geographical references, and sagas. There is a classical emphasis in the work that is illustrated with black-and-white drawings and concludes with a list of Greek and Roman names, a selected bibliography, and a general index.

Grant, Michael, and John Hazel. *Gods and Mortals in Classical Mythology.* Springfield, Mass.: G. & C. Merriam, 1973. 447p.

Following the introduction is an alphabetical listing of significant personages in classical mythology. Completing the volume are maps, genealogical trees of the relationships among the gods, and a list of Greek and Latin words. The work is illustrated with photographs of paintings and sculpture.

Grimal, Pierre. *Larousse World Mythology.* Tr. by Patricia Beardsworth. New York: Putnam, 1965. 560p.

This one-volume work contains chapters on prehistoric religion, the mythologies of the ancient empires, India, China, Japan, Siberia, the New World, and Africa, as well as the Celtic, Germanic, and Slavic peoples. There is a suggested reading list that has divisions that parallel the chapter headings of the main text and the volume concludes with a general index. There are over thirty pages of color plates and numerous black-and-white illustrations.

Guerber, Hélène Adeline. *Myths of Northern Lands, Narrated with Special Reference to Literature and Art.* New York: American Book Co., 1895. 319p.

This one-volume work contains twenty-eight chapters discussing Norse cosmology, gods, legendary races, mythological events, and a comparison of Greek and northern mythologies. The volume is illustrated with black-and-white plates and concludes with an index to poetical quotations, and a general index that contains a pronunciation guide.

Poignant, Rosyln. *Oceanic Mythology: The Myths of Polynesia, Micronesia, Melanesia, Australia.* London: Hamlyn, 1967. 141p.

This extensively illustrated volume, written in a popular style, is geographically divided into sections dealing with the islands of the Pacific and Australia. Each division discusses cosmology, the gods of the people, mythological events and certain religious issues. The work concludes with a reading list and an index with geographical, personal, and subject entries.

Sacred Books

Müller, Max, ed. *The Sacred Books of the East.* New York: Dover, 1963–69. 50v.

This set was originally published in 1879. It contains translations of and scholarly introductions to the scriptures of Brahmans, Buddhists, Confucians, Jains, Muslims, Taoists, and Zoroastrians.

DICTIONARIES AND ENCYCLOPEDIAS

Gaskell, George Arthur. *Dictionary of All Scriptures and Myths*. New York: Julian Pr., 1960. 844p.

Gaskell attempts to convey the underlying meaning of terms related to the religious life and works through all time. A unifying thesis of the work is that there is a sacred language common to all faiths that becomes manifest in different forms. Most entries contain not only a definition but also exemplary quotations from relevant scriptures or writings about them. Cross-references and terms of related interest are also indicated at the end of each entry. Gaskell stresses a higher and unified meaning to all scripture and mythology partially to resolve what he views as the sterile conflicts and debates between defenders of a theistic cosmology and people with other points of view.

Particular Religions

AFRICAN RELIGIONS

BIBLIOGRAPHY

Ofori, Patrick E. *Black African Traditional Religions and Philosophy: A Selected Bibliographic Survey of the Sources from the Earliest Times to 1974*. Nendeln, Liechtenstein: KTO Pr., 1975. 421p.

This bibliography includes sources on Africa south of the Sahara and is divided into sections on Africa in general, West Africa, Central Africa, East Africa, and South Africa. These sections are further divided into subsections for the national entities. Under the national entity the entries are listed under tribal unit. The volume concludes with a list addenda, a list of journals, and author and ethnic indexes. The entries are taken from English, French, and German sources from the period up to 1974. Books, pamphlets, journal articles, theses, and dissertations are included.

BUDDHISM

BIBLIOGRAPHY

A Bibliography on Japanese Buddhism. Ed. by Brando Shojun et al. Tokyo: CIIB Pr., 1958. 180p.

This classified bibliography lists 1,660 articles and books in ten categories:

general; Shōtoku Taishi; Hossō, Jōjitsu, Kusha, and Sanron Sects; Kegon Sect; Ritsu Sect; Tendai Sect; Shingon Sect; Jōdo and Shin Sects; Zen Sects; and Nichiren Sect. After each bibliographic citation Japanese libraries possessing a copy of the item are noted. The volume concludes with an author and subject index.

Hanayama, Shinsho. *Bibliography on Buddhism.* Tokyo: Hukuseido Pr., 1961. 869p.

This bibliography contains unannotated citations for books, journal articles, and dissertations on Buddhism published in European languages. Authors are listed in alphabetical order with their works listed in chronological sequence, with each work receiving its own identification number. An index to titles appears at the end.

Vessie, Patricia Armstrong. *Zen Buddhism: A Bibliography of Books and Articles in English, 1892–1975.* Ann Arbor, Mich.: Univ. Microfilms International, 1976. 811.

This work was "published under the aegis of the East Asia Library of the University of Washington" (title page) and contains 762 entries divided topically. Part 1 deals with general works, historical development, texts, commentaries, and Zen sects. Part 2 deals with the interaction of Zen with such subjects as archery, the arts, Christianity, food, philosophy, and science and concludes with sections on Zen training, Zen and the West, and Zen periodicals. There is no index and the entries have no annotations except for selected content notes.

Yoo, Yushin. *Books on Buddhism: An Annotated Subject Guide.* Metuchen, N.J.: Scarecrow, 1976. 251p.

Yoo has divided his annotated bibliography into a series of form and subject headings, such as bibliographies, fiction, juvenile literature, ethics, Lamaism, missions, philosophy, and ritual. Within each section, the works are arranged alphabetically by author. Only books published in English are included; but some 1,300 are listed. Yoo has also written an introduction that sets forth the major events in the life of Buddha and the major principles of Buddhism. Author-editor-translator and title indexes are included. The book constitutes a companion to Yoo's *Buddhism: A Subject Index to Periodical Articles in English, 1728–1971,* published in 1973.

———. *Buddhism: A Subject Index to Periodical Articles in English, 1728–1971.* Metuchen, N.J.: Scarecrow, 1973. 162p.

This work is introduced by an essay on the history and teachings of Buddhism. The bibliography proper consists of unannotated citations to periodical articles in English arranged in alphabetical order by author under such subject headings as doctrine, history, meditations, schools, and sociology. At the end is a geographically arranged, international directory of Buddhist associations. A list of the periodicals indexed and title and author-subject indexes conclude the work.

DICTIONARIES AND ENCYCLOPEDIAS

A Dictionary of Buddhism. New York: Scribner's, 1972. 277p.

This work represents a compilation of entries dealing with Buddhism extracted from Brandon's *A Dictionary of Comparative Religion.* It is addressed to those persons who wish a brief but broad introduction to Buddhism as well as to those who specialize in Southeast Asian studies. Given the growing Western interest in this Asian religion, this dictionary is a useful, concise reference tool. The cross-references, indicated by arrows, also expand the opportunities for further study and broader knowledge of a given topic and its interrelationships. Doctrines, schools, treatises, states of being, historic sites and personages, mythology, and literary genres are all explained in a lucid manner. The topics are frequently explored in a comparative framework and are followed by references for further reading.

Humphreys, Christmas. *A Popular Dictionary of Buddhism.* New York: Citadel, 1963. 223p.

Humphreys introduces this work with an essay on the development of Buddhist thought and the spread of the movement. He has attempted to provide a compromise between a dictionary and an encyclopedia. Entries are generally briefer than in *A Dictionary of Buddhism,* but they contain explicit and implicit cross-references. Neither work consistently covers more terms than the other. Humphrey's work is also addressed to the person who has some knowledge of the field but who is not a scholar in it. Entries deal with doctrines, states of being, important persons and places, societies, and other terms essential to an understanding of the religion. Occasionally, a work for further reading is noted. This dictionary is a useful tool, and Humphreys brings conciseness and order to a vast field in which translation and transliteration difficulties are especially acute.

Malalasekera, G. P., ed. *Encyclopedia of Buddhism.* Ceylon: Government of Ceylon, 1961– .

This multivolume work was begun in 1961 and is still in process. It is being published in fascicles at the rate of approximately one a year. The articles, which are normally signed, are written by international scholars who are usually Buddhists. The encyclopedia is addressed both to the expert and to the general reader and aims at comprehensiveness, containing information on both the Mahāyāna and Theravāda schools. When differences of opinion exist, there may be more than one article on a subject. In sum, the origins and development of Buddhism around the world are examined in depth with attention to such topics as doctrines, schools and sects, rituals, the fine arts, and biographies. The arrangement is alphabetical, which aids in the serial format for publication but is inconvenient for examination of some of the larger topics, which are subdivided and scattered. A comprehensive index is designed to ameliorate some of these difficulties.

Soothill, William Edward, and Lewis Hodous, comps. *A Dictionary of Chinese Buddhist Terms, with Sanskrit and English Equivalents and a*

Sanskrit-Pali Index. London: Kegan Paul, 1937. Repr.: Taipei: Ch'eng-Wen, 1968. 510p.

This dictionary provides definitions in English of Chinese Mahayana Buddhist terms. The terms are arranged first by strokes and then by radicals with an index of classification by strokes, a list of radicals, and a list of characters with difficult radicals appearing before the dictionary proper. The volume concludes with an index of Sanskrit and Pali terms and with an index of other terms.

SACRED BOOKS

Sacred Books of the Buddhists. Tr. by various Oriental scholars. London: H. Frowde; Oxford: Oxford Univ. Pr., 1895–1974. 30v.

These English translations of Buddhist texts are heavily annotated with explanatory footnotes and each translation is preceded by an introductory chapter discussing the structure of the work, its relationship to other texts, and concepts central to the understanding of the work. An index of Pali proper names follows each translation.

CHRISTIANITY

ARCHEOLOGY

Negev, Avraham, ed. *Archaeological Encyclopedia of the Holy Land.* New York: Putnam, 1972. 354p.

The editor of this work was a senior lecturer in classical archaeology at Jerusalem's Hebrew University when the work was prepared; the other contributors hold similar positions in institutions of higher education and in museums. The entries are of two principal types. Most are for place names appearing in the Bible. The sites are identified, and any excavations that have been carried out there and the significance of the discoveries are also treated. Thus, entries are to be found for Masada, Lachish, and Petra among many others. The second type of entry is designed to provide background information on the sites and to illuminate the culture and living conditions of the peoples occupying them in pre- and postbiblical times as well as during biblical times. The entries in this range cover such topics as musical instruments, water supply, money, and agriculture. Photographs are numerous. The main text is supplemented by a glossary, a list of ancient sources used in the compilation of the volume, and chronological tables.

ATLASES

Freitag, Anton. *The Universe Atlas of the Christian World: The Expansion of Christianity through the Centuries.* London: Burns & Oates, 1963. 200p.

Through maps, photographs, and text, this work portrays the history of the spread of Christianity during periods of growth and of retrogression. Chronologically, the work begins with the earliest efforts of the church during Roman times; it proceeds through the missionary efforts of Catholics and Protestants alike in Asia, the Pacific islands, and the world at the time of Vatican II. The maps portray ecclesiastical territorial divisions, routes of missionaries, and locations of missions and associated institutions. Notes on the illustrations and a general index appear at the end.

Littell, Franklin H. *The Macmillan Atlas History of Christianity*. New York: Macmillan, 1976. 176p.

This atlas focuses on tracing the history of Christianity through important encounters and confrontations between it and other civilizations, faiths, and ideologies. The texts, maps, and assorted other illustrations are organized into chronological chapters dealing with such subjects as the Jewish matrix of Christianity, disintegration of the Carolingian Empire, European Christendom in the age of colonialism, the great century of Christian missions, and the ecumenical movement. Some space is also devoted to the cultures and ideas themselves that have confronted Christianity. The maps vary in size and amount of detail but are abundant. A general index is appended.

Van der Meer, F. and Christine Mohrmann. *Atlas of the Early Christian World*. London: Nelson, 1958. 216p.

This work is divided into two principal sections. The first contains forty maps, and the second contains texts and photographs dealing with the early Christian world from the first through the seventh centuries. The maps show locations of churches, early Christian writers, monuments, cemeteries, pilgrimages, monasteries, and martyrdoms. The texts contain many quotations from early Christian writers while the photographs portray sculpture, mosaics, archaeological sites and many other items in their attempt to describe early Christian life. At the end are notes on the maps and a geographical index as well as an index to authors and inscriptions.

BIBLIOGRAPHY

McLean, George F. *A Bibliography of Christian Philosophy and Contemporary Issues*. New York: Frederick Ungar, 1967. 312p.

This bibliography provides unannotated citations to books and articles published during the thirty-year period preceding its compilation. Works are listed under major and minor subject headings, such as philosophy and technology, contemporary atheism and the death of God movement, religious languages, and the teaching of Christian philosophy. An appendix lists dissertations written at Catholic universities in Canada and the United States. An index appears at the end.

O'Brien, Elmer. *Theology in Transition: A Bibliographical Evaluation of the "Decisive Decade," 1954–1964*. New York: Herder & Herder, 1965. 282p.

This work consists of signed essays on theological issues with a lengthy bibliography appearing at the end of each. The essays treat theological trends, Old and New Testament studies, patristic studies, liturgical studies, and theology in transition. At the end are notes on the contributors, and subject and name indexes.

Union Theological Seminary. *Catalogue of the McAlpin Collection of British History and Theology.* Comp. and ed. by Charles Ripley Gillett. New York: The Seminary, 1927–39. 5v.
These volumes list those works, including books and pamphlets, in the McAlpin collection at the time the catalog was published. Many works have been acquired and added since that time. No annotations are provided. Books are arranged within each volume first according to the year of publication and then alphabetically by author. The four main volumes cover respectively the years 1500–1640, 1641–52, 1653–79, and 1680–1700, with the final volume being an index.

―――. Library. *Alphabetical Arrangement of Main Entries from the Shelf List.* Boston: G. K. Hall, 1960. 10v.
This ten-volume work is fairly accurately described by its title; listings from the McAlpin Collection of British history and theology, the Missionary Research Library, and the collection of general theological periodicals are omitted. The work is a key guide in many ways to the most outstanding collection of theological materials in the Western Hemisphere.

Williams, Ethel L., and Clifton F. Brown. *The Howard University Bibliography of African and Afro-American Religious Studies, with Locations in American Libraries.* Wilmington, Del.: Scholarly Resources, 1977. 525p.
This bibliography contains major divisions for the African heritage; Christianity and slavery in the New World; black religious life in the Americas; the Civil Rights Movement, 1954–67; and the contemporary religious scene, as well as numerous subdivisions. The works, both primary and secondary, are arranged alphabetically by author within each subdivision. Annotations are provided when titles are not self-explanatory. A code indicating at least one library location for each work is also provided. Appended are bibliographies of manuscripts and of biographies and autobiographies. An author index is included.

―――, comps. *Afro-American Religious Studies: A Comprehensive Bibliography with Locations in American Libraries.* Metuchen, N.J.: Scarecrow, 1972. 454p.
This bibliography lists books, periodical articles, and other more ephemeral publications that deal with Afro-American religious studies. The work is divided into major and minor subject areas with the citations appearing in alphabetical order according to author within these areas. The major divisions are the African heritage, Christianity and slavery in the new world, the American Negro and the American religious life, the civil rights movement, and the contemporary religious scene. If the title is not indicative of the contents, a brief annotation is provided. Each citation is followed by a letter code indicating one or more libraries where the work is located. Appendixes

list relevant periodicals and serials and manuscript collections. An author index concludes the volume.

DICTIONARIES AND ENCYCLOPEDIAS

Cross, F. L., and E. A. Livingston, eds. *The Oxford Dictionary of the Christian Church.* 2d ed. London: Oxford Univ. Pr., 1974.

The second edition of this volume updates and expands an already comprehensive and scholarly volume which is, nevertheless, intended for the educated layperson. The editors have written approximately one-half of the material, and the remainder has been contributed by other authorities. Other faiths that have had some bearing on Christianity are also examined. The dictionary includes doctrines, movements, bodies, events, holidays, and places and is strong on biography. Few entries are devoted to the Bible because this topic is covered amply in other reference sources. Each article normally ends with a list of key works for further reading. In addition, asterisks within the text indicate other related articles. The editors of this edition have given special attention to particular councils and changes in policy resulting therefrom and to the Eastern Church in their revisions of the 1958 volume. The text is preceded by a lengthy list of church-related abbreviations.

O'Brien, T. C., ed. *Corpus Dictionary of Western Churches.* Washington: Corpus, 1970. 820p.

The primary emphasis of this work is on the institutional history and characteristics of Christian churches in the Western tradition with special attention to those of North America. The tone is ecumenical and factual rather than polemical. One purpose of the book is to encourage dialogue among all Christians about churches other than their own and to promote an understanding of underlying unity. To this end, a wide range of theologians and scholars with varying backgrounds have contributed to the work. The articles also deal with doctrine, practice, and personalities in so far as they relate to church history. A church is defined loosely as a body with a distinct set of beliefs and practices as well as some organization. Short bibliographies are often appended to the articles, and cross-references are indicated by asterisks and/or small capitals. The work is prefaced by a useful list of abbreviations treating documents as well as common terms.

Purvis, J. S. *Dictionary of Ecclesiastical Terms.* London: Nelson, 1962. 204p.

This work is addressed primarily to the English general reader and student who wishes a better understanding of the meaning of ecclesiastical terms. In general, words that are rare or antiquated, are exclusively Greek and of concern only to the Eastern Orthodox church, or are strictly personal and biographical are omitted. The length of the entries ranges from a line to a few paragraphs. The entries treat such subjects as general categories of persons (e.g., bishop coadjutor), specific groups (e.g., Dominicans), physical locations, implements, symbols, law and duties, scriptures, and doctrines.

White, Richard C. *The Vocabulary of the Church: A Pronunciation Guide.* New York: Macmillan, 1960. 178p.

This work contains exactly what its title indicates and nothing more or less. It is a guide for the non-expert and is intended to supplement and draw together pronunciation information from other reference sources. Each word entry is followed by a simple and straightforward phonetic pronunciation. The work is oriented toward an American audience and utilizes pronunciations commonly accepted by the American public. If these differ from the original foreign language pronunciations, the American usage predominates, if it is widely known. The book includes person and place names from the Bible and church history; and if the standard biblical texts differ, variant pronunciations are noted. Also included are doctrinal and ecclesiastic terms as well as those from the modern jargon of other disciplines if they relate to the church. Not included are terms widely used and on which there is no question of pronunciation. Nor are certain technical Latin and Hebrew terms included.

DIGESTS

Magill, Frank N., ed. *Masterpieces of Christian Literature in Summary Form.* New York: Harper & Row, 1963. 1,193p.

This volume is a collection of summaries of 300 works dealing with Christian devotion, history, and philosophy. The Protestant viewpoint is stressed with approximately two-thirds of the works examined originating after the Reformation. The arrangement is chronological with writers from St. Clement and Aristides to Pierre Teilhard de Chardin and Gerhard Ebeling represented. For each selection, the author's dates, the type of work, the date of first publication, and the principal ideas advanced are noted in addition to the provision of a 2,000-word summary. An alphabetical list of titles, a category index, and an author index are included.

ETHICS

Macquarrie, John, ed. *Dictionary of Christian Ethics.* Philadelphia: Westminster Pr., 1967. 366p.

This work represents an attempt to cull the essential concepts of various aspects of Christian ethics. Because it is intended in part as a beginning point for future study, bibliographies are frequently provided at the ends of the signed articles. Most of the contributors held academic positions and/or high ecclesiastical posts. Various viewpoints are in evidence. In addition to treating Christian ethics per se and questions of universal concern under such entries as St. Augustine of Hippo, choice, evolutionary ethics, and justice, other ethical systems, such as those providing source material for or influencing Christian ethics, are also covered. Entries range in length from a paragraph to several columns.

FATHERS OF THE CHURCH

The Ante-Nicene Fathers: Translations of the Writings of the Fathers down to A.D. 325. New York: Christian Literature Co., 1896. 10v.

These volumes contain the writings of and notes on the lives of the church fathers who wrote before the First Council of Nicaea in 325. Bibliographical and explanatory footnotes are provided to aid scholars, church persons, and the laity. Indexes may be found in each volume as well as in the final volume, which also provides an extensive bibliography.

Schaff, Philip, ed. *A Select Library of the Nicene and Post-Nicene Fathers of the Christian Church.* Buffalo, N.Y.: The Christian Literature Co., 1886. 14v.
————, ed. *A Select Library of the Nicene and Post-Nicene Fathers of the Christian Church, Second Series.* New York: Christian Literature Co., 1890. 14v.

These two sets were compiled to provide reasonable access to the patristic literature of the Christian church. The first series contains translations of the writings of and information on the lives of St. Augustine and St. Chrysostom. The second series begins with the *Church History* of Eusebius and continues to John of Damascus and Gregory the Great. The final volume of the second series contains the texts of the early ecumenical councils. The writings are accompanied by extensive bibliographical and explanatory footnotes. Indexes appear at the end of each volume.

HISTORY

Brauer, Jerald C., et al., eds. *The Westminster Dictionary of Church History.* Philadelphia: Westminster Pr., 1971. 887p.

The emphasis of this dictionary is on institutional church history and within that on the modern period, beginning with the eighteenth century, in America. The work is geared to the educated layperson, the student, and the clergy. Most articles are limited to concise, factual description and range from ten to thirty lines. Only the longer entries add bibliographical references. Historical events and personalities receive more attention than ideas. Only a few entries on the Bible are included because this topic receives wide coverage in other reference sources.

Jedin, Hubert, and J. Dolan, eds. *Handbook of Church History.* New York: Herder & Herder, 1965–80. 5v.

This series, translated from the German, is intended to describe the main events and personalities in the history of the Christian church and to present the development of the church's ecclesiastical doctrine, liturgy, dogma, organization, and literature. Following a comprehensive introduction to the subject the first volume covers such topics as Jewish Christianity, pagan religion at the time of the birth of the Christian church, the development of Christian literature in the third century, Manichaeism, and the Diocletian

Persecution. Succeeding volumes treat church history in detail. An index and selected bibliographies are included in each volume.

Neill, Stephen; Gerald H. Anderson; and John Goodwin; eds. *Concise Dictionary of the Christian World Mission.* Nashville, Tenn.: Abingdon Pr., 1971. 682p.
Over 200 contributors have assisted in producing this encyclopedia that deals with the spread of Christianity throughout the world since 1492. The three types of signed entries are for geographical place names, such as Colombia and Rhodesia; for persons, such as Father Damien; and for general subjects, such as the history of missions, lay missioners, social changes, and team ministries. Most of the entries contain cross-references and are capped by short bibliographies.

HYMNOLOGY

Diehl, Katherine Smith. *Hymns and Tunes: An Index.* New York: Scarecrow, 1966. 1,185p.
Diehl has provided a multifaceted guide for locating hymns and their tunes. The book is introduced by an essay and then is divided into five major parts. These sections are indexes of first lines and variants, authors and first lines, tune names and variants, composers and tune names, and a systematic, coded index to melodies. The first and third parts provide citations to the hymnals in which the work may be found. The appendixes include, among other things, a glossary, a bibliography, and a survey of hymnals.

Julian, John, ed. A *Dictionary of Hymnology, Setting Forth the Origin and History of Christian Hymns of all Ages and Nations.* New York: Dover, 1907. 2v.
This work tells the history of hymns, especially those in German, English, Latin, and Greek, in that order. It also has articles on national and denominational hymnody. It provides biographical, doctrinal, devotional, and ritual details.

McDormand, Thomas Bruce, and Frederic S. Crossman. *Judson Concordance to Hymns.* Valley Forge, Pa.: Judson Pr., 1965. 375p.
This work contains 2,342 hymns from 27 hymnbooks representing those of major denominations of the United States and Canada. Youth hymnals and gospel songbooks are included. An enumerated table of first lines arranged alphabetically comprises the body of this volume. A line index using key words provides further access.

Parks, Edna D. *Early English Hymns: An Index.* Metuchen, N.J.: Scarecrow, 1972. 168p.
This work serves as a finding list for early English printed hymns and also as a source of some information about their provenance. The hymns are listed in alphabetical order by the opening line. Subsequent information includes the meter, number of stanzas in the original, the author, and the

name, date, and page of the source where the hymn may be found. At the end is a bibliography as well as author, composer, and tune indexes.

ICONOGRAPHY

Child, Heather, and Dorothy Colles. *Christian Symbols Ancient and Modern: A Handbook for Students.* New York: Scribner's, 1971. 270p.

This work is addressed not only to students but also to artists and crafts-persons seeking explanations and inspirations. The symbols dealt with are those found in the decorative and applied crafts, such as carving, embroidery, stained glass, and mosaics. The symbolism inhering in some architectural plans is not treated. Black-and-white photographs and line drawings abound. The text is divided into categories, such as the cross, the Trinity, water, angels, good and evil, evangelical symbols, animals, and work and time. An index provides access to those items that are examined in several places. A brief bibliography is appended.

Ferguson, George. *Signs and Symbols in Christian Art, with Illustrations from Paintings of the Renaissance.* New York: Oxford Univ. Pr., 1959. 123p.

This work gathers together information from several disparate sources on representative signs and the more deeply significant symbols associated with Christian art up to the Renaissance, when signs and symbols were at their height. Divided into topical sections, such as the saints or fauna and flora, it is also well indexed. There are some additional sections on biblical and early Christian life. The book contains a wealth of color and black-and-white plates as well as line drawings and depends to a large extent on the illustrations. It is easily read without being simplistic and would be of interest to all age groups.

Roeder, Helen. *Saints and Their Attributes, with a Guide to Localities and Patronage.* Chicago: Regnery, 1955. 391p.

Roeder has compiled a guide to the iconography of saints and the symbols associated with them in art. The saints are listed alphabetically under one or more categories, such as arrows, key, archangels, fish, and star. Dates, positions, and place of birth are noted for each saint as well as details on their representation and notes on their attributes and habits. Finally, information is provided on their patronage and on the localities where they are venerated. Indexes of saints, patronage, and localities are included. At the front of the book are a few sketches illustrating typical modes of dress.

Sill, Gertrude Grace. *A Handbook of Symbols in Christian Art.* London: Cassell, 1975. 241p.

Sill's concise encyclopedia provides explanations for many of the images used as symbols and themes in Christian art. The arrangement is alphabetical, with some entries subdivided. Topics include angels, kings, color, vestments, prophets, and the Trinity, among many others. Reproductions of artistic works are abundant, as are references to scriptural passages. A bibliography and an index are included.

LITURGY

Davies, John G. *A Dictionary of Liturgy and Worship*. New York: Macmillan, 1972. 385p.
The articles give definitions, historical backgrounds, and relationships to the contemporary scene. They provide the rationale of worship, the tracings of patterns and influences, and underlying bases, and include terms from the world's religions. The articles have been written by experts from the various churches, and are treated in historical order.

NAMES

Withycombe, E. G. *The Oxford Dictionary of English Christian Names*. 3d ed. Oxford: Clarendon Pr., 1977. 310p.
This work gives a brief history of the origins of an alphabetic list of English Christian names that have been in use since the end of the fourteenth century, or were revived later. Some of the more common Irish and Welsh names are included. Each entry notes the earliest recorded form of the name with reference to the original source; a brief history of the use of the name; pronunciation, if doubtful; and cross-reference to variant forms. The original sources referred to in the entries are noted in the List of Abbreviations. A supplement has "Some Common Words Derived from Christian Names."

SAINTS

Farmer, David Hugh. *The Oxford Dictionary of Saints*. Oxford: Clarendon Pr., 1978. 435p.
This biographical dictionary of the saints of Great Britain has entries for all the saints recorded in English place names, in the Calendar of the Book of Common Prayer, the Sarum Rite, and the Calendar of the Roman Church as revised in 1969. The most important and representative saints of Ireland, Scotland, and Wales are also included. Arranged alphabetically by Christian names for those who lived before the sixteenth century and by surname thereafter, brief biographical sketches are followed by bibliographic citations. An appendix lists thirteen persons considered saints although never canonized. An "Index of Places in Great Britain and Ireland Associated with Particular Saints" is an added feature.

THEOLOGY

Dictionaries and Encyclopedias

Harvey, Van A. *A Handbook of Theological Terms*. New York: Macmillan, 1964. 253p.
Harvey is interested in increasing the quantity and quality of dialogue

between professional theologians and laypersons. He has, therefore, provided a word book designed to give explanations rather than mere definitions of terms used in systematic and philosophical theology. He normally omits other types of theological terms, such as those used in liturgies or in ethical discussions. His stress is on Protestantism and Roman Catholicism and the differences between them, with scant attention paid to the Eastern Orthodox positions. Most of the explanations contain cross-references and also attempt to provide some unity by clustering concepts.

Rahner, Karl, ed. *Encyclopedia of Theology: The Concise Sacramentum Mundi.* New York: Seabury, 1975. 1,841p.

Rahner and his scholarly colleagues have compiled a one-volume, ready-reference tool for the educated layperson interested in theological issues related to contemporary society. Many of the articles have been taken from the *Sacramentum Mundi, Lexikon für Theologie und Kirche,* and *Theologisches Taschenlexikon,* which are more comprehensive works ordinarily beyond the financial resources of the nonspecialist. New articles have been written in appropriate areas. The emphasis is on ideas and their related movements.

In addition to information on theological topics, the authors have provided entries on current topics of universal human and secular importance. Specialized terminology is employed only where essential. Articles are signed, often divided by appropriate subtopics, and contain numerous scriptural references. When appropriate, non-Christian religious and other sources are utilized. Textual references to these works are provided, although no bibliography per se is included.

Richardson, Alan, ed. *A Dictionary of Christian Theology.* Philadelphia: Westminster Pr., 1969. 364p.

Richardson has coordinated the efforts of thirty-six American and British scholars to produce a work in which the chief concerns are theology and philosophy and their interrelationships. Biblical and ethical topics are not treated here unless they have special relevance for theology, because they are examined in extensive detail in other sources. Christian ideas and their historical developments, rather than biography or events, are the focal points of this volume. A brief sample of topics includes being; Christology; the death of God theology; the liturgical movement; Blaise Pascal; Philo; repentance; the Social Gospel movement; and transubstantiation. The work is elucidating for both the general reader and the person with more education in theology. The value of each article is increased by the cross-references, indicated in bold-face type, and by the bibliographies.

BIBLE

Animals

Møller-Christensen, V., and K. E. Jordt Jørgensen. *Encyclopedia of Bible Creatures.* Philadelphia: Fortress, 1965. 302p.

The animals dealt with in this book are entered alphabetically under categories for mammals, birds, insects, and mollusks, fish, reptiles, and worms. The short articles explain the roles of the animals in the Bible and how they were perceived. Footnotes at the beginning of each article provide information on zoological classifications and transliterations of the Hebrew and Greek words used in the Bible. Illustrations are plentiful. An appendix provides brief notes on minor animals. Indexes of creatures, of names and places, and of scriptural references are included.

Atlases

Baly, Denis. *Geographical Companion to the Bible.* New York: McGraw-Hill, 1963. 196p.

The first and major portion of this book describes biblical lands and places in context the events and activities that happened on them. Included, for example, are sections on northern Syria, agricultural products, and battles. Several maps are interspersed. Other portions contain colored plate maps, photographs, and a dictionary of place names. An index to biblical references and an index to the text are appended.

Grollenberg, Luc H. *Atlas of the Bible.* Paris: Elsevier, 1956. 158p.

This work, with integrated maps, text, and photographs, takes a chronological approach beginning with the Fertile Crescent and the patriarchs and concluding with the political situation at the time of the birth of Jesus and with Palestine in the time of the Apostles. Boundaries, battles, travels, censuses of the tribes, and locations of memorable events are all dealt with in detail through the tri-pronged approach. At the end is an index of personal and place names.

May, Herbert G., ed. *Oxford Bible Atlas.* 2d ed. London: Oxford Univ. Pr., 1974. 144p.

This work is based both on biblical references and on archaeological finds. The maps illustrate such places and events as the Exodus, the United Monarchy, David and Solomon, the Babylonian Empire, and Jerusalem in New Testament times. Almost all of the maps are accompanied by a brief text that ties the map to biblical data and to the important extra-biblical context. Most of the maps are in relief although some are schematized to show vegetation, rainfall, and city street layouts. An introduction on Israel and the nations and a concluding essay on archaeology and the Bible lend coherence and a broader scope to the work. Both essays contain many photographs of archaeological sites and artifacts. The gazetteer at the back provides both identifying phrases and map citations. When necessary, variant forms of the name and cross-references are also noted.

Negenmann, Jan H. *New Atlas of the Bible.* Garden City, N.Y.: Doubleday, 1969. 208p.

This work contains maps, photographs, and text employed in an integrated fashion. These elements are combined in a series of chapters that trace the development of the Bible as history and its thematic contents. A general index is included.

Rowley, H. H. *Dictionary of Bible Place Names.* Old Tappan, N.J.: Revell, 1970. 173p.

From Abana to Zuph, Rowley has attempted to set forth the main biblical and some extra-biblical information relating to place names found in the Revised Standard Version, including the Apocrypha, of the Bible. A few variant names found in the Jerusalem Bible have also received attention. Scriptural references and cross-references are plentiful. Appended are maps of the ancient Near East, Palestine in Old and New Testament times, the journeys of St. Paul, and Jerusalem in the time of Christ.

Wright, George Ernest, and Floyd Vivian Filson. *The Westminster Historical Atlas to the Bible.* Philadelphia: Westminster Pr., 1956. 130p.

In addition to maps basic to biblical study, this work has explanatory chapters that provide a historical background for the Scriptures. It also has photographs. It has an index to the text as well as a gazetteer.

Bibliography

Anderson, G. W., ed. *A Decade of Bible Bibliography: The Book Lists of the Society for Old Testament Study, 1957–1966.* Oxford: Blackwell, 1967. 706p.

This volume consists of ten yearly book lists, each divided and published under twelve subject areas. For each book included, full bibliographic information and price are provided as well as a substantial and critical annotation. The annotations are initialed, and a key to these is provided at the front of the book. The subject areas include general works, education, archaeology and epigraphy, history and geography, text and versions, exegesis and modern translations, literary criticism and introduction, law, religion and theology, the life and thought of the neighboring peoples, the Dead Sea Scrolls, the Apocrypha and post-biblical Judaism, and philology and grammar. An author index concludes the volume.

Bible Bibliography 1967–1973: Old Testament. The Book Lists of the Society for Old Testament Study, 1967–1973. Oxford: Blackwell, 1974. 505p.

The society's lists actually contain signed, critical annotations of monographic works on the Old Testament. Each yearly list is divided into categories for general works; archaeology and epigraphy; history and geography; text and versions; exegesis and modern translations; literary criticism and introduction; law, religion, and theology; the life and thought of the surrounding peoples; Qumran studies; Apocrypha and post-biblical studies; philology and grammar; and additional notes on school textbooks, etc. Within each category, the arrangement is alphabetical by author. Prices are noted in addition to bibliographic information. An author index is included.

France, R. T., ed. *A Bibliographical Guide to New Testament Research.* Cambridge: Tyndale Fellowship for Biblical Research, 1974. 45p.

This work is addressed primarily to British students who are beginning New Testament studies. The format is a mixture of briefly annotated citations, commentary on methodology, and bibliographic essay. The emphasis is on background sources and those areas particularly difficult to approach. The chapters include such subjects as Greek Lexica, periodicals, topography, the Septuagint, Philo and Josephus, and early Christian and Gnostic literature.

Hester, Goldia, comp. *Guide to Bibles in Print.* 3d ed. Evanston, Ill.: Schori, 1970. 35p.

This guide emphasizes Bibles published in English in the United States, although some foreign language editions are included as well. The main divisions are for whole Bibles, the Old Testament, the Apocrypha, and the New Testament with subsequent arrangement by translation, text edition, and/or reference edition. Final subdivisions are for type size and the use of rubrics, and arrangement within these is alphabetical by publisher and then by ascending price. At the end are a list of Bible reference books and a directory of publishers.

Hurd, John Coolidge, Jr., comp. *A Bibliography of New Testament Bibliographies.* New York: Seabury, 1966. 75p.

Hurd's bibliography is divided into major sections for selective book lists, historical and chronological surveys, comprehensive (research) bibliographies, and New Testament scholars: biographies and bibliographies. The third section is the most extensive and contains subdivisions for the New Testament as a whole, for individual books, for New Testament words, for special subjects or areas, and for related areas of study. Many of the citations have been given brief but evaluative annotations. The arrangement of bibliographies within each section is chronological with the most recent appearing first.

Rowley, H. H., ed. *Eleven Years of Bible Bibliography: The Book Lists of the Society for Old Testament Study, 1946–56.* Indian Hills, Colo.: Falcon's Wing Pr., 1957. 804p.

This volume consists of eleven yearly book lists, first arranged chronologically by year, then by subject area, and finally by author. For each book included, full bibliographic information and price are provided as well as a substantial and critical annotation. The annotations are initialed, and a key to these is provided at the end of the book. The subject areas included are the Apocrypha and post-biblical Judaism, archaeology and epigraphy, the Dead Sea Scrolls, education, exegesis and modern translations, general history and geography, law, religion and theology, life and thought of the neighboring people, literary criticism and introduction, philology and grammar, and text and versions. Subject and author indexes conclude the volume.

Commentaries

The Anchor Bible. Garden City, N.Y.: Doubleday, 1964– .

The Anchor Bible is being produced for the general reader and reflects international and interfaith scholarship among Catholics, Jews, and Protestants. Each volume is divided into short sections of text that are followed by specific explanatory notes and then by a commentary.

Black, Matthew, and H. H. Rowley, eds. *Peake's Commentary on the Bible.* London: Nelson, 1962. 1,126p.

This work is based on the text of the Revised Standard Version as well as on other English-language versions when they have been deemed appropriate. The contributions have been drawn from scholars from Britain, the Commonwealth, and the United States. The articles are of two principal types. Some treat general subjects, such as the geography of Palestine; weights, measures, money, and time; archaeology; the doctrine of the church in the New Testament; and the synoptic problem. The others contain the usual type of analyses of the themes and meanings of the chapters of the books of the Bible. A general index and maps, with a gazetteer, appear at the end of the volume.

Brown, Raymond E., et al., eds. *The Jerome Biblical Commentary*. Englewood Cliffs, N.J.: Prentice-Hall, 1968. 2v. in 1.
This work is by Catholic scholars and reflects the ecumenical attitude generated by the Second Vatican Council. It is also based on the emphasis on biblical scholarship that Catholicism has encouraged in recent years. Thus, it uses historical and literary criticism in its treatment of passages. There are topical articles as well as commentary.

Buttrick, George Arthur, et al., eds. *The Interpreter's Bible*. New York: Abingdon-Cokesbury Pr., 1951–57. 12v.
The 125 exegetes and expositors include many of the best biblical scholars. At the top of the page the passages in the King James Version and the Revised Standard Version are given. Midway on the page is the exegesis, which gives the settings of phrases and the meanings of words. The expositions give the meaning of the passages for the present time.
Each book also has an introduction, which deals with the authorship, date, and historical situation in which the passage was written, and which includes an outline of the book and a bibliography. The set also includes general articles and maps.

Fuller, Reginald C., et al., eds. *A New Catholic Commentary on Holy Scripture*. London: Nelson, 1969. 1,377p.
This work utilizes modern biblical research by Catholic writers. It reflects the ecumenical spirit of the Second Vatican Council, and is based primarily on the Revised Standard Version. The commentary is on paragraphs rather than on verses. It has articles of introduction and includes maps and an index.

Grant, Frederick C., ed. *Nelson's Bible Commentary*. New York: Nelson, 1962. 7v.
These volumes include the biblical text of the Revised Standard Version and the Apocrypha on the upper part of each page with notes and commentary that explain language, customs, and historical events on the lower part. Introductions to each book and references for additional reading supplement the commentary.

Harvey, A. E. *The New English Bible: Companion to the New Testament*. n.p.: Oxford Univ. Pr., Cambridge Univ. Pr., 1971. 850p.

Harvey examines the books of the New Testament and offers historical and exegetical comments for each on a line by line basis. He also places the lines and his comments in a larger context when appropriate and attempts to show relationships. He takes into consideration various viewpoints and presents a balanced, scholarly analysis. In addition, he has written a brief introduction to the New Testament and to each of its major subdivisions. When appropriate, he refers the reader to other portions of the Bible. The biblical text used is that of the *New English Bible.*

Laymon, Charles M., ed. *The Interpreter's One-Volume Commentary on the Bible.* Nashville, Tenn.: Abingdon Pr., 1971. 1,386p.

The contributors to this volume are biblical scholars, and they have addressed their material to students and laypersons as well as to ministers and other professional persons. The work is divided into nine parts. The first through third portions provide exegeses for the Old and New Testaments and the Apocrypha on a verse-by-verse basis. The fourth section contains general articles on such topics as the Fertile Crescent and its environment, the Hebrew community and the Old Testament, and languages of the Bible. The fifth and sixth parts deal respectively with chronology and with measures and money. The seventh section contains an index to scriptural references, the eighth contains over fifteen plate maps, and the ninth is a subject index. Sketch maps and other illustrations also appear occasionally throughout the text. All articles are signed.

Neil, William. *Harper's Bible Commentary.* New York: Harper & Row, 1962. 544p.

This work is not an exegetical one but rather a series of essays designed to lend coherence and understanding to those persons engaged in biblical study.

Concordances

The Computer Bible. Ed. by J. Arthur Baird and David Noel Freedman. Wooster, Ohio: Biblical Research Assoc., 1971– . v. 1– .

The *Computer Bible,* based on Greek and Hebrew texts, is designed to provide solutions to the problem in biblical research of gathering new data, handling vast amounts of critical information effectively, and treating such data as objectively as possible. An international team of scholars, using computers, is organizing and indexing critical data on the Bible, to make it readily retrievable for scholars and students. Analytical concordances include analysis of morphology, syntax, style, linguistic phenomena, and semantic data, plus problems of form, source, audience, redaction, and linguistics.

Cruden, Alexander. *A Complete Concordance to the Old and New Testament.* London: Frederick Warne, n.d. 719p.

This work indicates the biblical chapters and verses where both common and proper words may be found. It also provides definitions for proper names and for those common words with multiple or obscure meanings. Additional features include lists of the names and titles given to Jesus and to the Church, together with scriptural citations, a concordance to the Apocrypha, and summaries of the books of the Bible.

Darton, Michael, ed. *Modern Concordance to the New Testament.* Garden City, N.Y.: Doubleday, 1976. 788p.

This work, which is compatible with several modern translations of the New Testament, is intended to allow the reader or researcher to find most of what is written in the New Testament on a subject. It is not arranged like most concordances but is arranged into "themes" that group related words. Under "Gathering," for example, are included such words as "church," "congregation," and "assembly." The occurrences of "hard" in the sense of "difficult," for instance, are also separated from those of "hard" as in the expression "hard-hearted." An index provides access for those who wish to use the volume to locate a particular verse. The organization of the themes was based in part upon the Greek. The Greek equivalents of the English words are given, and an index of Greek words also is provided.

Ellison, John W., comp. *Nelson's Complete Concordance of the Revised Standard Version Bible.* New York: Nelson, 1957. 2,157p.

This book was produced through the use of a Univac I computer at the offices of Remington Rand, Inc. It locates most of the words and phrases of the Revised Standard Version, omitting a few very common words, such as "it" and "up." The key word in each phrase is abbreviated to its initial letter, followed by a period.

In using a concordance it is usually best to look up a phrase under its least common word. Under a given heading the order is that of the books of the Bible as given in the Revised Standard Version.

Hartdegen, Stephen J., ed. *Nelson's Complete Concordance of the New American Bible.* Nashville, Tenn.: Nelson, 1977. 1,274p.

This concordance to the 1970 New American Bible translated by Catholic scholars has more than 300,000 alphabetic entries covering 18,000 key words. Notations next to each word heading give book, chapter, and verse in which it can be found as well as sense quotations to aid further study.

Strong, James. *The Exhaustive Concordance of the Bible.* New York: Abingdon Pr., 1967. 1,340p., 262p., 126p., 79p.

The main portion of this volume is an alphabetical listing primarily of nouns, adjectives, verbs, and adverbs with citations to and quotations from the biblical passages where they occur. An appendix provides briefer references to such common words as "a," "of," and "that." Strong based this concordance upon the King James Version but provided a comparative concordance to indicate differences in words and phrasing in the Revised Version. The third and fourth sections provide dictionaries of Hebrew, Chaldean, and Greek words.

Thompson, Newton, and Raymond Stock. *Complete Concordance to the Bible (Douay Version).* St. Louis: Herder, 1945. 1,914p.

This volume is an alphabetical list of words, except such common ones as "to be," "which," and "of," appearing in the Douay, a Catholic version of the Bible. The citations to the passages and excerpts from them appear directly after the work listed.

Young, Robert. *Analytical Concordance to the Bible.* . . . 22d American ed. rev. by William B. Stevenson. New York: Funk & Wagnalls, 1955. 1,090p., 93p., 23p., 51p.

The main portion of Young's concordance contains about 311,000 nouns, adjectives, verbs, and adverbs in one alphabetical order with the corresponding scriptural passage(s) noted as well as a definition(s) of the word and transcriptions of the original Aramaic, Greek, and Hebrew words when relevant. The index-lexicons to the Old and New Testaments provide definitions of Aramaic, Greek, and Hebrew terms and indicate parallel passages. The third portion of the volume is a pronunciation guide to proper names in the Scriptures. The final section on discoveries in biblical lands deals primarily with specific geographical locations, such as Samaria, Egypt, and Persia but also contains a chapter on research methodology and a chronological table.

Dictionaries and Encyclopedias

Barker, William P. *Everyone in the Bible.* Westwood, N.J.: Revell, 1966. 370p.

Biblical persons, from the best known to the most obscure, are identified in this work. The entries are usually brief, consisting of one or two sentences; but in the case of important figures such as Jesus, Peter, and Moses, they can run to a page or more. The information given includes who the individual was, to whom he or she was related, any important events with which he or she was associated, and citations to biblical verses in which the person is mentioned. When two or more people have the same name they are clearly distinguished. The Revised Standard Version was used in writing this work, but there are cross-references from common variant spellings.

Brownrigg, Ronald. *Who's Who in the New Testament.* London: Weidenfeld & Nicolson, 1971. 448p.

Directed to the layperson and general reader, this volume identifies and assesses the significance of people mentioned in the New Testament. Included are both proper personal names and names of certain political and religious groups. Derivations of the names from Hebrew, Greek, or Latin are frequently provided as are references to and quotations from scriptural passages. Some of the persons included are Bernice, the Corinthians, Nicodemus, Judas of Galilee, Zenas, and tax collectors. The volume is profusely illustrated with photographs and maps.

Cornfeld, Gaalyahu, ed. *Pictorial Biblical Encyclopedia: A Visual Guide to the Old and New Testaments.* New York: Macmillan, 1964. 720p.

Incorporated in this one volume are articles reflecting twentieth century biblical research, illustrated by many photographs and maps. The articles deal with such topics as the Dead Sea Scrolls, magic, divination and superstition, feasts and festivals, Nabateans, the Temple, Babylonia, books of the Bible, and many other topics. Explanations of the illustrations are included in the text (instead of as captions). An index is provided.

Gehman, Henry S., ed. *New Westminster Dictionary of the Bible*. Rev. ed. Philadelphia: Westminister Pr., 1970. 1,027p.

This work includes pronunciation. The biblical quotations have been taken from the Revised Standard Version. Insights from archaeology and historical studies have been introduced; the work includes photographs, drawings, and detail maps.

Hartman, Louis F. *Encyclopedic Dictionary of the Bible: A Translation and Adaptation of A. van den Born's Bijbels Woordenboek, 2d rev. ed., 1954– 57.* New York: McGraw-Hill, 1963. 2,634p.

Hartman has relied heavily on the Dutch original of this work, his principal changes involving the substitution of a more recent or agreed-upon explanation in some cases or of sources and explanations more meaningful to American and English audiences. The work is prefaced by synchronized chronological tables for Palestine, Syria/Northern Mesopotamia, Egypt, Babylonia, Assyria, and Eastern Asia Minor. The entries include such topics as geographical place names, persons (both individuals and classes), institutions, doctrines, customs, deities, and scriptures. They contain definitions and word derivations as well as discussions replete with scriptural references. These discussions range from a paragraph to several columns. Photographs, drawings, and maps supplement the text.

Hastings, James, ed. *Dictionary of the Bible*. Rev. ed. by Frederick C. Grant and H. H. Rowley. New York: Scribner's, 1963. 1,059p.

This dictionary is based on the Revised Standard Version of the Bible. It is strong on biblical persons and places.

The Interpreter's Dictionary of the Bible: An Illustrated Encyclopedia. New York: Abingdon Pr., 1962. 4v.
———. Supplement. 1976. 998p.

This work includes articles on proper nouns, important objects, and theological terms from the Bible. It also has terms from the Pseudepigrapha, pseudonymous writings that purport to have been written by biblical characters; the Apocrypha; and deuterocanonical books, writings outside the canon of the Old and New Testaments. There are articles on the Dead Sea Scrolls; historical backgrounds of Sumer, Babylonia, Assyria and Egypt; peoples of the ancient Near East; flora; fauna; arts; cities; crafts; the calendars; archeology; pottery; and governments. It has an introduction to each biblical book and to such concepts as redemption, atonement, love, and resurrection. Each major article has a bibliography, and many have outlines. Etymologies are given, and the volume includes maps, charts, and photographs. The supplemental volume revises articles in areas where new knowledge has been gained and includes additional articles on topics not covered in the original work.

McKenzie, John L. *Dictionary of the Bible*. London: Chapman, 1972. 954p.

This volume identifies persons, places, events, and concepts appearing in the Bible. For many of the terms, McKenzie, a Jesuit, has provided not only a definition but also an indication of their significance and of relationships.

Thus, one finds brief identifications of Phygelus and Raamah but longer discussions of the Qumran scrolls and soul. Photographs appear throughout the volume, and a general bibliography has been printed at the front of the work.

Miller, Madeleine B., and J. Lane Miller. *Harper's Bible Dictionary.* 7th ed. New York: Harper & Row, 1961. 854p.

This work provides identifications and brief discussions of persons, places, objects, and concepts appearing in the Bible. Some of the longer articles are initialed by their authors. Photographs and line drawings appear frequently and bibliographic references occasionally. At the back are several plates of maps showing the political boundaries of Palestine and neighboring countries during different epochs and routes taken in various journeys. A map index accompanies the plates.

Guides and Handbooks

Asimov, Isaac. *Asimov's Guide to the Bible.* Garden City, N.Y.: Doubleday, 1968–69. 2v.

Asimov has attempted to provide an historical guide to the Bible for the general reader. His intention was to elucidate historical references in the Bible and also to illuminate historical events and persons by examining what the Bible had to say about them. Each book, including the Apocrypha, is examined in turn with explanations of concepts, persons, places, animals, and so forth. The approach is informal and varies as Asimov deems appropriate. Maps are interspersed throughout the text. A chronology is appended, and indexes of biblical verses and of subjects are included.

Blair, Edward P. *Abingdon Bible Handbook.* Nashville, Tenn.: Abingdon Pr., 1975. 511p.

Blair has sought to meld scholarship and Christian devotion in his guide, which is addressed to those persons who have difficulty in understanding the Bible. The book is divided into three principal parts. The first portion deals with the Bible today: its characteristics, versions, translations, and the origins thereof. The second part treats the Bible in history, first with a book-by-book approach and then with a background section on manuscripts and archaeology accompanied by tables and comments on measures, weights, money, festivals, and the calendar. The final portion is concerned with the Bible as it relates to faith and life. Photographs, maps, charts, and tables are valuable additions throughout the book, and an index appears at the end.

Corswant, W. *Dictionary of Life in Bible Times.* New York: Oxford Univ. Pr., 1960. 308p.

Addressed both to the teacher and the pupil, Corswant's work is based on scholarship but employs readily understandable language. It defines words dealing with domestic life, work, arts and sciences, political, civil, and military affairs, holy places, holy persons, sacred seasons, sacred acts, animals, plants, and minerals in biblical times. Cross-references and citations to biblical passages allow the reader to pursue further many subjects. Illustrations are plentiful. The arrangement is alphabetical, but a classified list of topics precedes the entries. The entries range in length from a few lines on the elephant to several columns on uncleanliness.

Finegan, Jack. *Handbook of Biblical Chronology: Principles of Time Reckoning in the Ancient World and Problems of Chronology in the Bible.* Princeton, N.J.: Princeton Univ. Pr., 1964. 338p.

How time was measured in the different civilizations of the ancient world and how it appears in the Bible are the major concerns of this handbook. Finegan divides his work into two main parts, the first dealing with principles of chronology in the ancient world, the second with problems of chronology in the Bible. In part one he discusses numerals, the reckoning of time in the ancient world, and early Christian chronographers, particularly the work of Eusebius. In part two he covers modern systems of biblical chronology, chronology of the Old and New Testaments, and the lives of Peter and Paul. The work also includes some 150 tables, a list of ancient sources, lists of abbreviations, an index of scriptural references, and a general index.

Kittel, Gerhard. *Bible Key Words.* Tr. and ed. by Dorothea M. Barton and P. R. Acroyd. New York: Harper & Row, 1951–64. 4v.

These volumes contain lengthy essays on the meanings of key words in the Bible and also, to some extent, in the surrounding cultures. The first volume deals with love, the church, sin, and righteousness; the second explores the words Lord, gnosis, *basileia,* and apostleship; the third, faith and spirit of God; and the fourth, law and wrath. Each subject area is examined in a number of signed, scholarly essays. Bibliographies and indexes to scriptural references are included for each subject word.

Richardson, Alan, ed. *A Theological Word Book of the Bible.* New York: Macmillan, 1959. 290p.

The contributors to this volume are scholars and members of the church hierarchy. They have presented signed discourses on the meanings of many biblical, theological, or doctrinal terms, including proper names when they have assumed theological meanings. The length of the entries ranges from a paragraph to several columns. Cross-references add unity and encourage further study, as do the occasional suggestions for further readings. The entries include such topics as blasphemy, grace, obedience, prophecy, and desire and the names of such persons as Abraham, David, and St. John the Baptist. The essays treat various meanings of the terms and include many scriptural references.

The World of the Bible. New York: Educational Heritage, 1959. 5v.

The five volumes of this series (*The Law, Former Prophets, Later Prophets, The Writings,* and *The New Testament*) are designed to give a pictorial view of the world of biblical times. Verses and quotations from the Bible are illustrated with colored plates of scenes in the lands of the Bible, ancient ruins, artifacts, seals, texts, steles, tomb decoration, temple reliefs, paintings, pottery, coins, statues, and relief maps. Brief commentaries accompany each verse and illustration. Indexes to the plates complete each volume.

History

Cambridge History of the Bible. Cambridge: Cambridge Univ. Pr., 1963–70. 3v.

The three volumes of this history, written by notable biblical scholars, trace biblical history from earliest times to the present. The first volume, edited by P. R. Ackroyd and C. F. Evans, covers such broad topics as language and script, books in the ancient world, the Old Testament, the New Testament, and the Bible in the early Church. The second volume, edited by G. W. H. Lampe, includes early Christian book production, Jerome, the exposition and exegesis of the Latin Vulgate, the "People's Bible," Bible illustration in Medieval manuscripts, and the vernacular Scriptures. Volume 3, edited by S. L. Greenslade, includes chapters on the Bible in the Reformation, biblical scholarship, continental versions of the Bible, English versions of the Bible, the Bible in the Roman Catholic church from Trent to the present day, and the printed Bible.

Each volume is illustrated with black-and-white plates. Bibliographies and a general index complete the set.

Indexes and Abstract Journals

Metzger, Bruce M., comp. *Index to Periodical Literature on Christ and the Gospels.* Leiden: Brill, 1966. 602p.

This bibliography provides a unified index to 160 periodicals published in sixteen languages. The articles are listed under six major subject areas and numerous smaller divisions. No annotations are provided. An author index appears at the end.

New Testament Abstracts. Cambridge, Mass.: Weston Coll. School of Theology, 1956– . v.1– .

These volumes provide summaries of journal articles of international provenance dealing with the New Testament. All abstracts are initialed, and a list of contributors may be found at the end of each issue. Unsigned book notices appear after the abstracts of periodical articles. The publication is issued three times a year.

Quotations

Stevenson, Burton E. *The Home Book of Bible Quotations.* New York: Harper & Row, 1949. 645p.

Stevenson's book has an alphabetical subject arrangement of quotations with a detailed index that is almost a concordance. The text is based on the King James Version and includes quotations from the Apocrypha. The subjects may be persons, such as Jonathan; places, such as Lydia; emotions, such as merriment; acts, such as eating; animals, such as goat; concepts, such as honesty, and so forth. Explanatory notes are occasionally added.

Texts

May, Herbert G., and Bruce M. Metzger, eds. *The New Oxford Annotated Bible: The Holy Bible, Revised Standard Version, containing the Old and New Testaments.* New York: Oxford Univ. Pr., 1973. 1,596p.

This edition of the Revised Standard Version of the Bible includes introductions to each book of the Bible and notes on the text contributed by many biblical scholars. Some special features include an index to the annotations, twelve indexed color maps, a table of measures and weights, and a chronological listing of rulers. Special articles deal with Hebrew poetry, modern biblical study, geography, history and archaeology of biblical lands, literary forms of the Gospels, and English versions of the Bible from Tyndale's to the King James.

Theology

Bauer, Johannes B., ed. *Encyclopedia of Biblical Theology.* London: Sheed & Ward, 1976. 3v. in 1. 1,141pp.

Originally a German work compiled by biblical scholars from Austria, France, Germany, and Switzerland, this encyclopedia consists of signed articles on terms with significance in biblical theology. The essays are addressed both to scholars and the laity and seek to explore changes in meaning of such words and phrases as retribution, servant of the Lord, mercy, freedom, image, and angel. At the end of each entry is a bibliography. The last volume contains a supplementary bibliography of books and articles published between 1967 and 1970, an analytic index of articles and cross-references, an index of biblical references, and an index of Hebrew and Greek words.

Kittel, Gerhard, ed. *Theological Dictionary of the New Testament.* Grand Rapids, Mich.: Eerdmans, 1964–76. 10v.

This set contains nine volumes that treat the meanings and significance of New Testament theological and religious terms as well as some important prepositions and numbers and a few Old Testament terms and names. The terms are given in their original Greek and are arranged according to the Greek alphabet. The entries attempt to provide more than a lexical definition but aim at less than a full exegetical commentary on the New Testament. Quotations are frequent and appear in the original Greek, Hebrew, or Latin. Many words are accorded more than one essay when meanings vary. Each entry is signed. The tenth volume contains indexes to English key words, Greek key words, Hebrew and Aramaic words, and biblical references. It also contains an identification of and index to the essays by the contributors. Because of the necessity for a background in ancient linguistics for using this work, it is of use chiefly to theological students and biblical scholars.

Leon-Dufour, Xavier, ed. *Dictionary of Biblical Theology.* 2d ed., rev. and enl. London: Chapman, 1973. 712p.

This work provides discourses, normally several columns in length, on theological and related terms appearing in the Bible. Scriptural references are frequent. The discussion for a given term may be divided into several sections if there are multiple meanings or varying significances. The topics include burial, king, messiah, redemption, and trial/temptation. Each entry is initialed, with a key to these appearing at the front of the volume. At the end are an analytic table of terms and an index.

PROTESTANT DENOMINATIONS

Guides, Handbooks, and Yearbooks

Mead, Frank S. *Handbook of Denominations in the United States.* Nashville, Tenn.: Abingdon Pr., 1975. 320p.

In narrative form, this gives historical, statistical, organizational, and doctrinal information on most of the sects in the United States.

Yearbook of American and Canadian Churches. New York: Abingdon Pr., 1916– .

This work provides directory information on religious bodies including denominations, ecumenical and international organizations, theological seminaries, church-related colleges, religious periodicals, and service agencies. Each entry provides the name and address of the group and the names of the principal officers. In the case of denominations, a brief, historical sketch is included. The *Yearbook* also has statistical information on church membership and finance. It has, in addition, a calendar of religious dates and a listing of depositories of ecclesiastical historical materials.

ROMAN CATHOLIC

Bibliography

CLA Booklist. Haverford, Pa.: Catholic Library Assn., 1942/45– .

Originally published under the title *Catholic Booklist,* this annual bibliography lists and annotates books by Catholic authors and/or about Catholic themes. Each issue is divided by such forms, subjects, and audiences as biography, fiction, mission literature, philosophy, religion, and high school. Within these sections, the arrangement is alphabetical by author. Author-title indexes for adult and juvenile books are included.

McCabe, James Patrick. *Critical Guide to Catholic Reference Books.* Littleton, Colo.: Libraries Unlimited, 1971. 287p.

This bibliography lists, and in many cases critically annotates, some 900 reference works that deal with Catholic subjects or that take a Catholic approach. Included are both English and foreign language publications, stressing books in print and available in libraries in the United States. The volume is divided into five major sections and numerous subject and form subdivisions. The first part deals with general reference works and the other sections with theology, the humanities, the social sciences, and history. An appendix lists diocesan reference publications. A list of bibliographies consulted and a general index conclude the volume.

Biography

Delaney, John J., and James Edward Tobin. *Dictionary of Catholic Biography.* Garden City, N.Y.: Doubleday, 1961. 1,245p.

This work contains concise biographical sketches on almost 15,000 Catholics who made what the editors deemed to be significant contributions to the Church or who were influential historical or cultural figures; living persons are excluded. The entries contain the persons' dates and places of birth and death, information on educations and careers, and notes on their significant contributions. Cross-references are supplied when necessary. At the end are lists by occupation and by place with their patron saints as well as a list of the symbols used in art to represent particular saints. These are followed by a chronological chart of popes and world rulers.

Dictionaries and Encyclopedias

Broderick, Robert C. *The Catholic Encyclopedia*. New York: Nelson, 1976. 612p.

Broderick has attempted to compile a broad-ranging one-volume encyclopedia for home and school that encompasses some of the new Catholic thinking and ecumenical approach, as exemplified in the article on the Jews, as well as new terms. The work is definitely Catholic in its views, as can be seen in such articles as the one on abortion. Individual biographies are rare, but entries for groups of persons, writings, doctrines, and movements tied to individuals abound. Other entries deal with such diverse topics as institutions and councils, rites, theological concepts, and places. Some articles include lists and tables. Several of the entries are accompanied by block-print style illustrations, and a few photographs are also included in groups.

The Catholic Encyclopedia Dictionary. New York: Gilmary Soc., 1941. 1,095p.

This dictionary, a condensation of the *Catholic Encyclopedia* by its editors, contains "8500 articles on the beliefs, devotions, rites, symbolism, tradition and history of the church; her laws, organizations, dioceses, missions, institutions, religious orders, saints; her part in promoting art, science, education and social welfare" (title page). Many of the entries are initialed, and contributors are listed at the back of the volume. Illustrations are plentiful. The book concludes with classified tables of contents.

McDonald, William J., et al., eds. *New Catholic Encyclopedia*. New York: McGraw-Hill, 1967. 15v.
————. ————. Supplement. 1974.

This work was prepared under the auspices of the Catholic University of America. It contains articles on literature, the arts, and the sciences in addition to ecclesiastical subjects. The stress of the work, however, is on the doctrine, organization, and history of the Catholic church in the English-speaking world. The encyclopedia has 17,000 articles by 4,800 contributors, including some non-Catholic scholars. The tone is ecumenical. It is strong on retrospective biography, and most articles have a bibliography. It has 7,500 illustrations, more than 300 maps, and an index.

Directories

The Official Catholic Directory. New York: Kenedy, 1817– .

This contains ecclesiastical statistics from the world. It gives the governing bodies in the Vatican City, the United States, statistics on religious orders, a list of places with Catholic institutions, a list of the hierarchy of the United States, an alphabetical list of the clergy, and a general recapitulation of sixty-three categories for each archdiocese and diocese.

Documents and Digests

Carlen, Sister Mary Claudia, comp. *Dictionary of Papal Pronouncements: Leo XIII to Pius XII (1878–1957).* New York: Kenedy, 1958. 216p.

This work provides summaries of and bibliographic details for papal encyclicals and a few other documents issued during an eighty-year period. These are arranged in alphabetical order according to the first few words of the text, which normally constitute the title. The condensations are indicative of the contents but do not explain or interpret. Other information provided includes date of publication or delivery, an indication of the type of document, a note on the audience to which the document was addressed, and a citation(s) to sources where the full text may be found. Following the dictionary proper are a list of papal document collections, a chronological list of documents under the various popes, and an index to personal and corporate names as well as to subjects.

Magill, Frank N., ed. *Masterpieces of Catholic Literature in Summary Form.* New York: Harper & Row, 1965. 1,134p.

Some 300 works, from the anonymous *Didache* to Pope John XXIII's *Pacem in Terris,* have been summarized in this volume. The works included are those the contributors and editors felt to have most influenced the development of Christianity. The contributors of the signed entries are or were scholars at Catholic universities. In addition to the summary, they have noted the author and her or his dates, the type of work, the date when first published, and the principal ideas advanced in each work. The arrangement is chronological with an alphabetical list of titles at the front of the volume. An author index is also included.

Guides, Handbooks, and Yearbooks

Catholic Almanac. Huntington, Ind.: Our Sunday Visitor, 1904– . Annual.

Similar in format to the *World Almanac,* this volume contains information on the Catholic church in the United States and on subjects of interest to American Catholics. There is a chronology of important events of the past year, a glossary, a brief biographical dictionary, and information on church doctrine and church activities in other countries. The *Almanac* also contains lists of churches and cathedrals, religious organizations, saints, and periodicals. Access is provided by an index at the front of the volume. Title varies.

History

Ellis, John Tracy, ed. *Documents of American Catholic History.* Chicago: Regnery, 1967. 2v.

Ellis has brought together documents that trace the role of the Catholic church in America from 1493 to 1966. Included are both official public documents, such as the Treaty of Tordesillas and the Act of Foundation for the First Permanent Trappist Monastery in the United States, 23 October 1848, and private, personal writings, such as Abbé Klein's "Impressions of Bishop McQuaid" (1903) and "George P. A. Healy Recounts His Beginnings as an Artist" and his painting of Pope Pius IX (1894). The documents are arranged chronologically under sections for the Spanish, French, and English colonies and the national period. Each document is preceded by an explanatory note. At the end of each volume is a comprehensive index to both volumes.

Indexes

The Catholic Periodical and Literature Index. Haverford, Pa.: Catholic Library Assn., 1930– .

This work is an author and subject index to books and periodicals relating to Catholicism or published by Catholic institutions. Brief descriptive annotations accompany the entries for books. Most of the periodicals indexed are in English, but a few French, Spanish, and Italian titles are included. Citations to reviews can be found under the headings "Book Reviews" and "Motion Picture Reviews." The work appears bimonthly, with two-year bound cumulations.

Liturgy

Podhradsky, Gerhard. *New Dictionary of the Liturgy.* Staten Island, N.Y.: Alba House, 1966. 208p.

Podhradsky has compiled an encyclopedic guide to the Catholic liturgy, dealing with meanings, origins, and reasons for changes as well as rules, law, dogma, and structure for such items as gestures, rituals, music, ceremonial objects, movements, and architectural features. A few biographical sketches are included as well. Photographs enrich the text, and a bibliography is appended.

Saints

Benedictine Monks of St. Augustine's Abbey, Ramsgate, comps. *The Book of Saints: A Dictionary of Persons Canonized or Beatified by the Catholic Church.* 5th ed. New York: Crowell, 1966. 740p.

This work provides information on the careers and significant contributions of canonized or beatified saints. In addition, when appropriate, it provides the surnames or distinctive appellations of the saints, as well as their hagiological ranks, liturgical membership groups, religious orders, the present state of their cult, feast day dates, and year of death.

Butler, Alban. *Butler's Lives of the Saints.* Ed. by Herbert Thurston and Donald Attwater. New York: Kenedy, 1963. 4v.

This work contains brief biographies of over 2,500 Catholic saints. The work has a calendar arrangement, with each saint's biography entered under his or her feast day. The articles concentrate on the religious aspects of the saints' lives, on their piety, martyrdom, or on other reasons for their having been canonized. Each volume is individually indexed, and a comprehensive index at the end of the last volume is included.

Theology

Dictionaries and Encyclopedias

Rahner, Karl, and Herbert Vorgrimler. *Theological Dictionary*. New York: Herder & Herder, 1965. 493p.

Rahner and Vorgrimler intended this work for the German educated layperson interested in Catholic dogmatic theology. The English translation is clear and faithful to the original, although English-speaking readers will in some instances find that topics of special interest to them are not included. The authors felt constrained by space considerations to omit bibliography and to write rather brief articles on historical topics. Concepts are, however, exposited clearly; and cross-references and references to scriptural passages, to conciliar documents of Vatican II, and to Denzinger add to the depth and breadth of the work.

HINDUISM

BIBLIOGRAPHY

Dandekar, Ramchandra Narayan. *Vedic Bibliography*. Bombay: Karnatak Pub. House; Pune, India: Poona Univ. of Poona, 1946– . v.1– .

This work is a classified, annotated bibliography that continues Louis Renou's *Bibliographie Védique* (Paris, 1931). The entries are written in Roman script with English annotations. Volume 1 has 3,500 entries from the period 1930–45; volume 2 covers 1946–60 and has 6,000 citations; volume 3, the largest volume, has entries from 1961 through the middle of 1972, as well as citations for items from the earlier periods that did not appear in volumes 1 or 2. Each volume contains a table of contents, which is the outline of the classified arrangement, and a list of journals cited preceding the main text. Each volume concludes with an author index and an index of key words.

CONCORDANCES

Bloomfield, Maurice. *A Vedic Concordance,* . . . Cambridge, Mass.: Harvard Univ. Pr., 1906. 1,078p. (Harvard Oriental ser., v. 10)

This work is an index to Vedic literature, liturgical formulae, and mantras and their variations in the different Vedic works. In the preface is contained a list of texts not included, and unpublished works that have been included. There is an extensive introduction detailing the use and entry system of the work followed by a listing of the works cited and the abbreviations used.

DICTIONARIES AND ENCYCLOPEDIAS

Dowson, John. *A Classical Dictionary of Hindu Mythology and Religion, Geography, History, and Literature.* 11th ed. London: Routledge & Paul, 1968. 411p. (Trubner's Oriental ser.)

This one-volume dictionary contains entries for Hindu deities, religious concepts, geographical terms, phrases, and historical personages. There are extensive cross-references, a Sanskrit index, and a general index. Preceding the text are an historical introduction and a guide to transliteration and pronunciation.

Walker, Benjamin. *The Hindu World: An Encyclopedic Survey of Hinduism.* New York: Praeger, 1968. 2v.

While a two-volume work cannot explore all the intricacies of this religion, Walker provides a concise, integrated tool for the beginning student. The articles deal with persons as well as concepts and events, and each identifies and defines key related terms. To increase the cohesion of the book, asterisks within entries indicate key cross-references and topics for further reading and study. In his translation of Sanskrit terms, Walker emphasizes meaning rather than ease of expression. Likewise, in his analysis of etymology, he stresses tradition rather than new interpretation if the latter would obscure an ancient concept. Bibliographies are appended to articles that may be several pages in length.

ISLAM

BIBLIOGRAPHY

Geddes, Charles L. *An Analytical Guide to the Bibliographies on Islam, Muhammad, and the Qur'an.* Denver: American Institute of Islamic Studies, 1973. 102p. (Bibliographic ser., no. 3)

This annotated bibliography has 211 entries in alphabetical order by main entry. The index is a single alphabetical arrangement of authors, coauthors, editors, compilers, titles, and subjects. Citations are from most European languages and Arabic, Persian, and Russian. All entries are in original script with a transliteration of the titles not written in roman script and English translations for items in "non-Western European languages" (intro). All annotations and content notes are in English.

Sauvaget, Jean. *Introduction to the History of the Muslim East: A Bibliographic Guide.* Based on the 2d ed. as recast by Claude Cahen. Berkeley: Univ. of California Pr., 1965. 252p.

This work on the history of Islam contains three sections: the sources of Muslim history; tools of research; and historical bibliography. The last section contains bibliographic essays on historical periods. An index of names completes the volume.

DICTIONARIES AND ENCYCLOPEDIAS

Gibb, H. A. R., et al., eds. *The Encyclopaedia of Islam.* New ed. Leiden: Brill, 1954– .
This eminently scholarly encyclopedia, prepared by a number of leading Orientalists under the patronage of the International Union of Academies, is a revision in progress of the 1913 edition. Not only does it provide more current information than its predecessor, but it also broadens its scope to include more entries on Islamic history, geography, and culture. Nevertheless, it will be necessary to use the two works in tandem until the second edition is complete. Articles range from a paragraph for minor biographical entries to several pages for major dynasties and movements. Entries begin normally with some etymological notes and conclude with bibliographical references. The work is quite comprehensive and provides information on the multitudinous aspects of Islam including its institutions, culture, and role in political, economic, and social history.

―――, and J. H. Kramers, eds. *Shorter Encyclopaedia of Islam.* Leiden: Brill, 1953.
This one-volume encyclopedia, edited on behalf of the Royal Netherlands Academy, is a condensation of the first edition of the five-volume *Encyclopedia of Islam* published in 1913. It contains only those articles, although normally in their entirety, dealing with Islamic law and religion. A scholarly work, it begins each entry by tracing the derivation of the word and then proceeds with an explanation of its meaning and the legal and religious importance throughout history of the concept, event, person, or object. Many entries are several columns in length and include bibliography, some of it new since the 1913 work. The work is fairly technical and designed for the person with some acquaintance with Islam.

INDEXES

London. University. School of Oriental and African Studies. Library. *Index Islamicus, 1906–1955: A Catalogue of Articles on Islamic Subjects in Periodicals and Other Collective Publications.* Comp. by J. D. Pearson. Cambridge: Heffer, 1958. 897p.
―――. ―――. Supplement, 1961–65. Cambridge: Heffer, 1967. 342p.
―――. ―――. Supplement, 1966–70. London: Mansell, 384p.
―――. ―――. Supplement, 1971– . London: Mansell.
This work includes articles published in Western languages, including Russian, in journals, as *Festschriften,* and as similar essays in collective works. Islamic studies in general are thoroughly covered under such headings as religion/theology, law, art, history, literature, and education. Numerous geographic and chronological subdivisions further categorize the material. A list of sources appears at the front and an author index at the back of the main volume and the supplements.

JUDAISM

ATLASES

Gilbert, Martin. *Jewish History Atlas.* n.p.: Macmillan, 1969. 112p.

Containing over 100 maps, this volume traces the key events and movements in the life of the Jewish people from the early migrations around 2000 B.C. to the post-World War II period. Historical, economic, political, and cultural developments are thus graphically illustrated. Each map, whether it shows the location of Hebrew printing presses, pogroms, or Israeli imports-exports, is accompanied by captions noting the import and context of what is displayed. There is no gazetteer, but there is a dictionary index of terms and themes with appropriate page references. A bibliography for further reading on some of the themes introduced in the atlas is appended.

BIBLE

Atlases

Aharoni, Yohanan, and Michael Avi-Yonah. *The Macmillan Bible Atlas.* Rev. ed. New York: Macmillan, 1977. 184p.

A total of 264 chronologically arranged maps depict the land of the Bible from ancient times to the second century A.D. The Revised Standard Version of the Bible is the source for quotations and geographic names. The findings of recent research and excavations have been incorporated. An appendix contains "Key to Maps According to Books of the Bible: Old Testament, Apocrypha, New Testament"; and "Chronological Table, General, Detailed." An index provides further access.

Commentaries

Kasher, Manahem M. *Encyclopedia of Biblical Interpretation: A Millenial Anthology.* New York: American Biblical Encyclopedia Soc., 1953– .

Nearly half of this thirty-five volume work has been translated into English. The translation has also somewhat condensed the original. It is a compendium of written and oral commentaries, including both parables and formal exegesis, on the Bible that have appeared from the time of Moses to the Gaonic or Talmudic-Midrashic period, with additional commentary on material from this last period. The first volume also contains appendixes with essays on such topics as the atom in Jewish sources and creation and human brotherhood. Each volume contains its own indexes.

Guides and Handbooks

Comay, Joan. *Who's Who in the Old Testament Together with the Apocrypha.* London: Weidenfeld & Nicolson, 1971. 448p.

Addressed to the general reader rather than to the scholar, this volume identifies and comments on some of the interpretative problems regarding persons, nations, and deities mentioned in the Old Testament and the Apocrypha. The entries for these books are in separate sections. Meanings of personal names are provided if the origin is reasonably clear. References to and quotations from scriptural passages are included. An introductory essay and a chronology provide a background setting for the textual entries. Some of the persons included are Tamar, Obadiah, Elijah, Uzziah, Mattathias, and Holofernes. The volume is profusely illustrated with photographs and maps.

BIBLIOGRAPHY

Berlin, Charles. *Index to "Festschriften" in Jewish Studies.* Cambridge, Mass.: Harvard College Lib.; New York: KTAV, 1971. 319p.

This volume indexes 243 *Festschriften* including all items published since 1937 and those earlier items not indexed in Marcus and Bilgray's *An Index to Jewish Festschriften* (Cincinnati, 1937). After the introduction is a listing of works included followed by an author index. The volume is completed by a subject index.

Brisman, Shimeon. *A History and Guide to Judaic Bibliography.* Cincinnati: Hebrew Union College Pr., 1977– . (Jewish Research Literature, v. 1)

This work is a classified guide to Judaic bibliographic books, monographs, and periodicals published through 1975. Detailed descriptive annotations also give historical background of the items cited. Chronological lists and summaries are located throughout the volume. Each of the eight classified sections is followed by notes for further study. An index provides further access. This volume is the first in a planned series of three, with encyclopedias to be covered by the second and the third devoted to dictionaries and concordances.

Celnik, Max, and Isaac Celnik, comps. *A Bibliography on Judaism and Jewish-Christian Relations.* New York: Anti-Defamation League of B'nai B'rith, 1965. 72p.

This bibliography lists and annotates almost 300 works, written primarily from a Jewish viewpoint, on Jewish history and culture and on Jewish-Christian interactions. It is addressed to scholars, librarians, and laypersons and includes only those books in print at the time of publication. The books are listed alphabetically by author under such headings as Talmudic literature; prayer, ritual, and festivals; Israel and Zionism; and music and art. Appendixes list some of the libraries where the books are available, Jewish periodicals, and addresses of publishers of the books. An author-title index concludes the work.

Harvard University Library. *Catalogue of Hebrew Books.* Cambridge, Mass.: Harvard Univ. Lib., 1968. 6v.

———. ———. Supplement. 1972. 3v.

These volumes reproduce the cards indicating the holdings in Harvard's Hebrew collection. The first volume of the supplement also lists Judaica works in the Houghton Library. The initial set divides its cards into four volumes for authors and subjects and two volumes for titles. The supplement divides its cards into three volumes. The first is a classified listing, the second has authors and selected subjects, and the third lists titles.

————. *Judaica*. Cambridge, Mass.: Harvard Univ. Lib., 1971. 302p. (Widener Library Shelflist, no. 39)

This volume lists those works on Judaica in two principal classifications that are possessed by the Widener and Houghton libraries of Harvard. The volume is divided into four parts. The first reproduces the classification schedules and acts as a table of contents. The second is a computerized reproduction of the shelflist. The third is a chronological list of works by date of publication; and the final section is an author and title listing. The volume is of use to researchers who wish to browse and ascertain the location of a particular title as well as to librarians in assessing their own collections.

Hebrew Union College. *Manuscript Catalog of the American Jewish Archives*. Boston: G. K. Hall, 1971. 4 v.

The American Jewish Archives preserves a large collection of materials relating the many aspects of the history and life of Jews in the Western Hemisphere, primarily in the United States. In addition to manuscript collections, documents, and typescripts, a body of ephemeral material is maintained. In three volumes of the published catalog are reproduced the author, title, and subject cards of these collections in one alphabet, including cross-references. The fourth volume of appendixes contains the catalogs of four notable collections housed in the archives. These are those of Louis Marshall, Jacob H. Schiff, Felix M. Warburg, and Jennie Franklin Purvin.

Lehmann, Ruth P. *Anglo-Jewish Bibliography, 1937–1970*. London: Jewish Historical Soc., 1973. 364p.

This work is generally based on and includes some of the references in Cecil Roth's older work, *Magna Bibliotheca Anglo-Judaica*. Books and articles are cited under numerous subdivisions dealing with such topics as Jewish history, education, culture, and bibliography in the British Isles and in the Commonwealth through various periods. Works are normally listed alphabetically by author although the subject matter occasionally dictates another arrangement. An index is included.

New York Public Library. Reference Department. *Dictionary Catalog of the Jewish Collection*. Boston: G. K. Hall, 1960. 14v.

————. The Research Libraries. *Dictionary Catalog of the Jewish Collection*. First Supplement. Boston: G. K. Hall, 1975. 8v.

These two sets reproduce the catalog cards that indicate the holdings of the Jewish collection of the New York Public Library. All works published before 1972 that deal with Jews and Judaism or that have been written in Hebrew, Yiddish, Ladino or in other languages using the Hebrew script have been included. Monographs, newspapers, and periodicals are all listed. Works published after 1972 are listed in the *Dictionary Catalog of the Research Libraries*.

Rosenbach, A. S. W. *An American Jewish Bibliography.* Baltimore, Md.: American Jewish Historical Soc., 1926. 500p. (Publication no. 30)

This bibliography cites books and pamphlets published from 1640–1850 that were written by or about Jews in America. It provides full bibliographic information, including collation details, as well as the library location(s) of the works. Title pages and excerpts have been plentifully reproduced. An author-title index appears at the back of the volume.

Shunami, Shlomo. *Bibliography of Jewish Bibliographies.* 2d ed., enl. Jerusalem: Magnes Pr.; Jerusalem: Hebrew Univ., 1965. 992p.

This work contains entries for over 4,700 bibliographies in sections devoted to encyclopedias, periodicals, and subjects such as religion, language, Bible, Talmudic literature, liturgy, and Yiddish, as well as historical periods and manuscript collections. The volume concludes with indexes for Hebrew titles, names, and subjects followed by the preface and list of contents in Hebrew.

The Study of Judaism: Bibliographical Essays. New York: KTAV for Anti-Defamation League of B'nai B'rith, 1972. 229p.

This work consists of six scholarly essays with bibliographies attached. The subjects treated are Judaism in New Testament times, rabbinic sources, Judaism on Christianity/Christianity on Judaism, modern Jewish thought, the contemporary Jewish community, the Holocaust, anti-Semitism, and the Jewish catastrophe. Both books and articles are included.

DICTIONARIES AND ENCYCLOPEDIAS

Ausubel, Nathan. *The Book of Jewish Knowledge: An Encyclopedia of Judaism and the Jewish People, Covering All Elements of Jewish Life from Biblical Times to the Present.* New York: Crown, 1964. 560p.

While Ausubel writes with a general Jewish viewpoint, he does not proselytize or espouse any particular doctrine or bias. He does not attempt to present a comprehensive encyclopedia dealing with all aspects of Jewish life, but rather concentrates on Jewish knowledge, learning, and thought: on the intellectual infrastructure of the Jewish community. He commences with a brief unifying essay on what he views as the particular character of this Jewish knowledge. The work contains extensive cross-references and an index and is rich in pertinent illustrations from historical and contemporary sources. The articles tend to be thorough yet concise. Biographies are not included, with the exception of Moses. Extensive references to key persons and explication of their thoughts and contributions, however, appear throughout the topical entries. In addition, there is a five-page section, "Some Architects of Jewish Civilization," which provides a brief sketch for each.

Encyclopedia Talmudica: A Digest of Halachic Literature and Jewish Law

from the Tannaitic Period to the Present Time Alphabetically Arranged.
Jerusalem: Talmudic Encyclopedia Inst., 1969– . v. 1– .

This encyclopedia, a translation from Hebrew, treats Halakhic subjects and subjects on which Halakha has some bearing. Thus one finds entries on such subjects as marriage, sale, and damages as well as on father and sunrise. The terms are arranged in order of the Hebrew alphabet with a Hebrew and English table of contents. The English edition provides some explanatory notes not found in the original but quotes fewer of the original sources by name. At the end of each volume is a subject index and a glossary.

Heller, Abraham Mayer. *The Vocabulary of Jewish Life.* Rev. ed. New York: Hebrew, 1967. 353p.

Designed for the layperson and the teacher, this book contains over 1,000 Hebrew terms with some spiritual content that Heller feels constitutes a basic vocabulary for contemporary Jews. A few Yiddish words are also included. The terms are entered and explained under categories, such as the synagogue, mourning, theological terms, and marriage and the family. A short essay introduces each section. In addition to definitions for the concepts, a transliteration and a guide to the Ashkenazic pronunciation are provided. An index to transliterations is included.

The New Jewish Encyclopedia. Ed. by David Bridger. New York: Behrman's, 1976. 541p.

This work provides concise information on Jewish life in a form useful to laypeople. The religion, history, culture, ethics, and literature of Jews are covered. Brief biographies of prominent Jews of all times and places are included. Numerous portraits, photographs, and other illustrations appear throughout the volume.

The New Standard Jewish Encyclopedia. New rev. ed. Ed. by Geoffrey Wigoder. Garden City, N.Y.: Doubleday, 1977.

This work is an update of *The Standard Jewish Encyclopedia,* 5th edition, which was published in 1959. The two emphases of the one-volume work are American Judaism and the State of Israel. Conciseness is the stated aim of the editor but there is an extensive use of cross-references. There are biographical and geographical articles as well as entries on Yiddish and Hebrew words and phrases, biblical books, and social customs. The articles are unsigned, but there is a list of contributors and their entries preceding the main text. Black-and-white photographs and drawings accompany many of the articles.

Roth, Cecil, et al., eds. *Encyclopaedia Judaica.* New York: Macmillan, 1972. 16v.
———. *Encyclopaedia Judaica Yearbook.* New York: Macmillan, 1975– .

This work is strongest on Jewish subjects but treats other people and topics that have influenced or been influenced by Judaism. It has capsule biographies and lists of outstanding Jews in various spheres. The biblical entries include orthodox and liberal interpretations. The set has 8,000 photographs, including several hundred in color. It also has maps, charts, and diagrams.

The yearbook chronicles the events of the previous year with an emphasis on Israel.

Werblowsky, Raphael Jehuda, and Geoffrey Wigoder, eds. *The Encyclopedia of the Jewish Religion.* New York: Holt, Rinehart & Winston, 1966. 415p.

This work utilizes a general encyclopedic approach but limits its scope to Jewish religion and religion-related topics. Given the particular orientation of Judaism, it includes folklore, law, and philosophy. Articles are concise but outline the key facets and contain cross-references for supplemental materials. Biographical sketches abound as well as entries on movements, customs, rituals, objects, festivals, groups, and doctrine. Where pertinent, relevant scriptural passages and Talmudic sources for further reading are cited. Another asset is the inclusion of several groups of plates from historic and contemporary sources.

Wigoder, Geoffrey, ed. *Encyclopedic Dictionary of Judaica.* New York: Leon Amiel, 1974. 673p.

Intended as a small-scale complement to the *Encyclopaedia Judaica* and published under the same auspices, the *Encyclopedic Dictionary of Judaica* contains brief factual entries and many supportive tables and illustrations in both color and black and white. Although written from a Jewish point of view, the dictionary avoids bias and value judgments in most cases. Its purpose is to identify the person, concept, object, or event and to place it in the Jewish historical-religious-cultural framework. The reader who is interested in pursuing a particular topic further at least knows where to begin and may then turn to other reference sources. The scope is comprehensive in terms of history and areas of the world. The tables and charts include information on such diverse topics as population, leaders and prize winners, dynasties, the Hebrew calendar, law codification, languages, coins, and a historical chronology.

GUIDES, HANDBOOKS, YEARBOOKS

American Jewish Year Book, 5660–. (Sept. 5, 1899–). Philadelphia: Jewish Pub. Soc., 1899– . v. 1– .

This work begins with signed articles on general subjects and the status of the Jewish community in the United States and other select countries which form the largest portion of the text. The remaining sections of the volume include a directory of Jewish organizations in the United States and Canada, a list of Jewish periodicals, a necrology, and an index with personal, organization, and subject entries.

Jewish Yearbook: An Annual Record of Matters Jewish. 5657–. (1896–). London: Jewish Chronicle, 1896– . v. 1– .

This work has a British emphasis and contains listings of Anglo-Jewish organizations followed by a selective international directory and a regional listing that includes synagogues, collegiate societies, youth centers, and a short statement of Jewish history for the United Kingdom. The volume concludes with a biographical section, an obituary, and a general index.

HISTORY

Bibliography

Brickman, William W. *The Jewish Community in America: An Annotated and Classified Bibliographic Guide.* New York: B. Franklin, 1977. 396p.

This bibliography covers the Jewish community in America from the colonial period to the present and contains 847 annotated entries divided into sections on history, sources and collections, autobiographies, biographies, community life, religious life, education, political and economic activity, immigration, anti-Semitism, periodicals and encyclopedias, and bibliographies. The entries are from English, Hebrew, Yiddish, Ladino, German, French, Hungarian, Polish, and Russian sources. There is a main entry index and an extensive appendix that includes letters, documents, and other primary and secondary sources on the history of the Jewish people in America.

Fluk, Louise R. *Jews in the Soviet Union.* New York: American-Jewish Comm., 1975. 44p.

This bibliography is a selective listing of sources, each with a short annotation, on Soviet Jewry from scholarly and popular writings published between January 1967 and September 1974 in English. The entries are divided into sections entitled bibliographies, periodicals, books and pamphlets, and articles. Subdivisions used within the sections are history, the current situation, the response abroad, and emigration. Author and subject entries are found in one index.

Marcus, Jacob R. *An Index to Scientific Articles on American Jewish History.* Cincinnati: American Jewish Archives; New York: KTAV, 1971. 240p.

This is an author, title, and to some extent thematic index to thirteen scholarly journals that publish articles on American Jewish life, history, and culture. The period covered is from 1884 through 1968.

Robinson, Jacob, and Philip Friedman. *Guide to Jewish History under Nazi Impact.* New York: Yivo Inst., 1960. 425p. (Jerusalem: Yad va shen. Joint documentary projects. Bibliographical ser., no. 1)

This volume contains over 3,800 entries in a classified arrangement with four main sections: the Jewish catastrophe in historical perspective; reference books; research; institutions methods and techniques; and documentation. Many of the parts have appendixes such as "General Works on the Third Reich" and "Totalitarianism." Concluding the volume are indexes for names, corporate authors, titles, defendants, places, and subjects.

Rosenberg, Louise Renee. *Jews in the Soviet Union: An Annotated Bibliography, 1967–1971.* New York: American Jewish Comm., 1971. 59p.

This work contains citations of 289 items from English-language sources divided into sections for periodicals, books and pamphlets, and articles. An index of names and places follows and the volume is concluded with a list of publishing organizations in the field.

Roth, Cecil. *Magna Bibliotheca Anglo-Judaica: A Bibliographic Guide to Anglo-Jewish History.* New ed., rev. and enl. London: Jewish Historical Soc. of England, 1937. 464p.

Roth, a historian, divided his bibliography into two main parts. The first contains histories of the Jews in England, the dominions, and dependences. It includes entries for biography and cultural history. The second part contains citations for what he termed historical material or those works primarily published before 1837. Here are listed proceedings of trials, grammars and dictionaries, almanacs, and works on the restoration to Palestine, among many others. A general index appears at the end.

INDEXES

Index to Jewish Periodicals. Cleveland Heights, Ohio: The Index, 1963– .

This is an author and subject index to periodicals relating to Jewish life and Judaism. It is issued semiannually. Journals of both a popular and a scholarly nature are covered.

ZIONISM

Dictionaries and Encyclopedias

Patai, Raphael, ed. *Encyclopedia of Zionism and Israel.* New York: Herzl Pr., McGraw-Hill, 1971.

This work was designed to fill a gap in reference sources by exploring important historical and current topics on Zionism and Israel and their interrelationships. Some 285 international scholars have contributed to the two-volume encyclopedia, which deals with Zionism in the Diaspora communities and in Israel. The work has biographical and place name entries as well as articles on such topics as historical events, ideologies, governmental agencies, ethnic groups in Israel, immigrants, and agricultural developments. Cross-references abound, and many pictures and tables complement the text. At the end of the second volume is an extensive topically organized bibliography.

Guides, Handbooks, Yearbooks

Zionist Yearbook. London: Zionist Federation of Great Britain and Ireland, 1951– .

This work includes the following features: a Jewish calendar, significant dates in Jewish history since 1 January 1827, a Zionist directory, and a general Jewish listing both with a British emphasis, a biographical section, an obituary, and some short articles including the year in review. A general index and a trade and commercial directory complete the volume along with an index to advertisers. Annual.

SHINTO

Holtom, Daniel Clarence. *The National Faith of Japan: A Study in Modern Shintō*. London: Kegan Paul; New York: Dutton, 1938. 329p. (Repr.: New York: Paragon, 1965)

This historical survey of Shintō is divided into sections covering State Shintō and Sect Shintō. These parts are subdivided into topical sections that are extensively footnoted. The general index contains personal and subject entries.

AUTHOR-TITLE INDEX

Compiled by Dickerson-Redd Indexing Systems

SUBJECT INDEX

Compiled by G. Fay Dickerson

189